PRAISE FOR CORPORATE REBEL

"I have long been a fan of the Corporate Rebels and this book captures the essence of their wisdom. The authors provide a no-nonsense, practical, and thought-provoking perspective on the world of work."
Daniel Pink, author of When, Drive, and A Whole New Mind

"Challenge chosen truth is one of my recurring mottos and that is exactly what Corporate Rebels are doing! A clever read for all employees, HR professionals and business leaders that want to create radically inspiring workplaces."
Katarina Berg, Chief HR Officer of Spotify

"Corporations need disrupting, and the business world needs the Corporate Rebels. They are a timely and very welcome wake up call for capitalism. A breath of fresh air in management thinking, the Rebels are on the Thinkers50 Radar for a very good reason. Their voices resonate for a new generation who are demanding a radically different approach to work and life."
Des Dearlove, co-founder of Thinkers50

"Businesses, or rather their customers and employees, are asking for more sustainable and better ways of organising work. The Corporate Rebels have been able to hit the nail on the head; they share alternatives in an inspiring way. Beautiful!"
Jos de Blok, founder and CEO of Buurtzorg

"A silent revolution in management is under way. For people to notice, and join the revolution, we need to give it a voice, or rather many, many voices. The Corporate Rebels have made it their job to bring us such voices and their stories."
Frederic Laloux, author of Reinventing Organisations

CORPORATE REBELS: MAKE WORK MORE FUN

ISBN 9789083004808
Cover and interior design VLERK&LIEM & Oranje Vormgevers
Copyright © Corporate Rebels Nederland B.V. 2019

CORPORATE REBƎLS

MAKE WORK MORE FUN

JOOST MINNAAR   PIM DE MORREE

LONDON

We straighten our bow ties. These suits take some getting used-to after leaving the corporate world behind years ago. The De Vere Grand Connaught Rooms serve the stage for today's Thinkers50 Awards Gala, also known as the Oscars of Management Thinking.

Leading figures of the management world are here: prominent academics, workplace gurus. We look slightly out-of-place. We're half the age of many of the other guests, and judging by the looks we get, we're not the only ones to notice.

While the presenter announces the nominees, we share a Corporate Rebels glance of amazement. Who would have thought we'd be at an event like this? When we started this adventure, nobody expected us to get this far. We had no money, no earnings model, and above all, no well-thought-out business plan. Our optimism brought us here.

We've visited five continents and more than 30 countries, investigated over 100 pioneers and conducted more than a thousand interviews. Based on this, we've written 300 blog posts, given presentations and helped companies to overhaul old-fashioned structures and working methods. We've been surfing in California while visiting one of these inspiring companies, where employees work for a better world. We've been to Stockholm to visit a company employing hundreds – but without a boss. We've spent time with a Chinese firm that has 70,000 employees who operate as if they're running their own business.

INTRODUCTION

PLUNGING IN

Ventura, southern California. It's 6:30am on a deserted beach off Highway 1, the lovely and meandering road we have been following for three weeks, stopping where the mood takes us. We roll out of the campervan and walk across the cold sand to the even colder waters of the Pacific Ocean, where two dolphins are playing, and a few early surfers are bobbing on their boards. In the half-light, we look out over the water. The morning couldn't be more beautiful – and here's the best part: we're here in our official capacity. It's a weekday, a workday, and just another day for Corporate Rebels.

We knew a long time ago that we wouldn't be stuck in steady jobs for 40 years. We craved something more. Something exciting. Something adventurous. What we didn't realise when we made the decision – months and miles away in Spain – was that escaping the corporate grind would be quite so easy; as easy as it is for those dolphins to flip out of a wave. Our real working life begins here, and man, it feels good.

In the summer of 2015, in a crowded beer garden in Barcelona, we talked about work – the work we were doing then. It was a rather sad conversation, because the bottom line was that our jobs were uninspiring at best. Work was making us anything but happy. Mondays to Fridays were spent counting down to the weekend, and that's not something anyone should be doing for 40 hours per week.

What made it worse was the fact that we weren't frustrated with the work itself. It was interesting, challenging, and a good fit for the engineering degrees we had completed. What was driving us nuts was the way our employers arranged things. That, and the fact that we were treated like children. There was no sense of freedom. The 9 to 5 mentality ensured that we were judged for the hours spent in the office, rather than what we did when we were there. It was frustrating to be forced to follow archaic and outdated procedures and protocols that held no room for creativity, offered no leeway. But what to do? Our corporate experience thus far entailed writing reports, which would disappear in a drawer to gather dust for a decade or two. There was a complete lack of appreciation for any sliver of lateral thinking or entrepreneurship. Any idea that might poke the status quo in the ribs was immediately shot down. We weren't experienced in the ways of business, but we knew we could set out on our own if we could just think what, exactly, we should do.

Ever since our university days we had been fascinated by pioneers, the brave souls who tackled "work" in a radically different way. We were inspired by companies that kept their employees engaged and connected. Our interest was sparked by a documentary about Brazilian entrepreneur Ricardo Semler. Semler made his machine factory, Semco, into a grand success in the 1980s by breaking rules and trashing all those conventions we had come to despise. Semco had no time for managers, unnecessary meetings, and pointless regulations. Employees had the freedom to determine their work hours – and their salary. We found more inspiration in the philosophies of workplace gurus such as Simon Sinek and Dan Pink. We dived into the extraordinary company cultures of Google and Spotify. There was a seemingly unbridgeable chasm between these inspiring stories and the drudgery of our day-to-day lives.

How did these progressive organisations function? What did they do differently, and how could others manage to make a change? Under the sunny skies of Barcelona, we reached a decision we have never regretted. And now, because of what we committed to then, over cervezas in Barcelona, we're here in Ventura, ready to plunge into the waves and our working life. We didn't do what our families, or society, expected of us. We quit our jobs with a vague but thrilling plan. We would travel the world, find the pioneers, and learn from them. Then we would share what they shared with us, in the hope that the message is heard.

Here's the message: Work can be fun. Work should be fun. I mean, just look at us, watching the sun come up in Ventura as the dolphin tussle in the waves, and surfers jockey for position. We're working, and it's wonderful. We're here to meet the first of our pioneers, to poke around in his brain and his soul and his management plan. But first we're going to dive into the water with him, and join the ranks of surfers waiting for that perfect California wave...

FROM COASTER TO COAST

Our bucket List began life as a Barcelona beermat, when we jotted down the names of those who inspired us. Naturally, Ricardo Semler was at the top of our list. But Richard Branson, Spotify, Simon Sinek, Google, and Dan Pink quickly followed. Our Bucket List became more refined with time, a list of progressive organisations, entrepreneurs, academics and writers who have something to teach the world about radically different ways of working. We wanted to see and speak to all of them and share everything that we learned on a blog.

We had to choose a name for ourselves and after kicking a few around, decided that Corporate Rebels not only sounded good, but also summed up our basic stance. By the time we left that Catalan beer garden, after a good few hours and a good few beers, we were convinced by the potential of our idea. And while we remained convinced, in the cold light of day, that the potential was real, not everyone agreed. Conversations with friends, family and colleagues tended to follow the same basic script:

"It all sounds wonderful, but how on earth will you make your money?"

We didn't really have a clue, so that was always a tricky one.

"So you're going to travel the world, searching for the most progressive organisations... but you don't know how you're going to make your money?"

That just about covered it. That was the plan. And while it was a wonderful idea, it wasn't a business plan. We didn't yet realise that wonderful ideas without business plans do not inspire much faith, but we discovered it soon enough. But hey, how could we focus on making money if we didn't even know anything about the topic? We

It was frustrating
to be forced
to follow archaic
and outdated
procedures and
protocols
that held no room
for creativity,
offered
no leeway.

opted to just start, learning from the best and figuring out what opportunities it would provide later. We were quietly convinced that the idea was sound. We believed in our purpose, our mission to make work more fun. Money wasn't our inspiration.

After we had pooled our savings, we calculated what we could do. We reckoned we had enough to cover ourselves for about 10 months. We'd have to change our lifestyle, because steady income would no longer be a thing. What was the worst that could happen? That our idea wasn't as good as we thought? That nobody was looking for the stories we would be sharing? That we discovered that we totally sucked at writing? That we would burn through our savings and have nothing to show for it? Those were all possibilities – but if they represented the worst that could happen... that's not too bad. We were privileged to have had a decent education, so if it went to the wall, we could always find other jobs. We would have gained some valuable experience. So, we added the figures up again, and found ourselves in agreement: This adventure wasn't entirely practical, but it was too good to pass up.

Shortly after the notion of Corporate Rebels was born, we handed in our notice, moved into a small apartment and lived together to save costs; we could no longer afford the luxury of two flats, and that room became the humble base for our embryonic project. For the next couple of months, everything we did, we did from there. We built our website, made plans for our Bucket List trips, read countless books on management, and started living the Corporate Rebels life.

We did the research and soon found out that we were not the only ones completely disengaged from work. Studies show that a lack of engagement with employees is a major issue all over the world. We were expecting this, but the reality is way worse than we thought. The research institute Gallup, which has been measuring employee engagement for years, and in over 150 countries, has come up with some numbers that shocked us. Worldwide, only 15 percent of employees feel engaged with the work they do. That means that the majority is disengaged every day. Within this group, there are employees who are so frustrated that they go out of their way to sabotage their workplace. These saboteurs make up 18 percent of the workforce. Studies in our native Netherlands have shown that just one in 10 employees is involved and engaged. Those statistics put us in the majority as part of the unhappy "niners" — along with our friends, our neighbours, our relatives, our parents. We discovered that we live in a world where the majority gets little or no satisfaction from their daily grind[1].

That only 15 percent of all employees are engaged at work is something that should be addressed. Although many organisations seem to be aware of this, it does little to spur them on to change. Which is strange, because Gallup estimates that globally, $7 trillion – more than half of China's GDP – is wasted in lost productivity thanks to disengagement. Despite this, the focus of traditional firms remains on performance, especially on money and output. Engagement is a nice-to-have, not a must-have.

We believed, and statistics and studies have proved, that a company with engaged employees will show better financial returns than a company staffed by unmotivated and unhappy people. Put yourself in the equation: you probably perform much better when doing things that you enjoy and find rewarding. It is simple. When work is exciting and motivating, people thrive and companies flourish. This is not just our belief – it is a verified fact proven by various surveys. A meta-study by Gallup highlights several positive influences on organisational success, showing that workplaces with high employee engagement seriously outperform the rest. Engaging workplaces enjoy significantly higher profitability, productivity and customer satisfaction. They also have lower staff turnover, less absenteeism and fewer accidents[2]. Moreover, the findings are highly consistent across organisations, industries and regions of the world. Not surprisingly, being on Glassdoor´s list of "Best Places to Work" (companies with the highest ratings from employees) is linked to superior financial performance. Investing in an engaged and inspired workforce doesn't just sound like a good idea, it most certainly is. Companies with well engaged employees really do outperform their peers. There is a direct correlation between a more engaged workforce and enhanced company performance[3][4][5].

In our little room we found one fascinating study providing compelling financial evidence: stock performance of progressive organisations based on three portfolios. A stock portfolio of public companies from Glassdoor's "Best Places to Work" list, one from public companies from Fortune's 100 "Best Companies to Work For" list and one based on the average of the overall S&P 500 market. The study shows that the stock portfolio of Glassdoor and that of the Fortune 100 substantially outperformed the overall S&P 500 market in five out of six years. For a robustness check, the researchers also looked at the returns among public companies with the lowest employee ratings on Glassdoor. They found that these companies broadly underperformed the S&P 500[6].

Now that we were convinced that having an engaged workforce is a very good idea, the next step was to find out how it is possible that most organisations still work in ways that create such a huge disengagement problem. We soon discovered that the laws of management obeyed in most of today's workplaces were created during the previous century. At school we learned the basic laws of physics and chemistry which were pretty much indisputable, but we now found that the laws of management are of a different sort: they all seem to be highly disputable. Management gurus seem to agree on one thing:

the history of the traditional laws of management. All modern texts tell more-or-less the same story. They point to Frederick Winslow Taylor, an early 20th century American who started the so-called Scientific Management Revolution and should take credit for the outdated principles which were developed during and after this revolution. For more than a century, Taylor and his ilk unleashed a quest for optimal workplace efficiency. The result is that most businesses still run on principles that are dated and hardly optimised for today.

In the 19th century, the world faced major problems in the workplace including staggering inefficiency, a gulf between poor workers and rich bosses, and an epidemic of worker disengagement. The workplace problems created tension. At one point there was a sort of Mexican standoff. This was a hot topic for the thinkers of the time. Everyone was talking about unavoidable workplace disruption. Karl Marx, for one, predicted a class war. He argued that suppression of the working class would inevitably lead to a revolution. Marx was right. The 19th century workplace problems did trigger a revolution, but of a totally different kind. What defeated these prophecies, was not the much-anticipated revolution of the frustrated working class, but the one started by Frederick Winslow Taylor.

In a nutshell, Taylor's book, *The Principles of Scientific Management*, argues that thinking work should be separated from doing work, with managers tackling the former. Taylor's theory is known as "the one best way". It advocates that every job should be reduced to a scientifically detailed, simple, repeatable and mechanical set of activities that any worker could understand. Taylor is followed by a number of other "bureaucrats" including Henri Fayol, a French mining executive who came up with the organisation chart; Henry Gantt, an American engineer, creator of the Gantt chart; Max Weber, a German economist, wrote on bureaucracy while Henry Ford introduced his famous assembly line. Over the next 100 years, Taylor's revolution spurred productivity in manufacturing and transportation in the developed countries by three to four percent a year. This explosive growth gave the working class increased incomes, access to education, healthcare, and opportunities for leisure. In fact, the revolution faired so well that today less than 10 percent of the world's population lives in extreme poverty versus more than 80 percent in Taylor's time. Nowadays, almost 90 percent has at least a basic education.

The bureaucrats still run the greater number of our modern-day workplaces. Most of our current organisational models find their roots in the industrial revolution and are based mainly on the ideas of Taylor et al. Their relentless pursuit of efficiency forced many organisations to squeeze out the highest productivity with the lowest possible expenditure of energy, time and money. Due to their efforts, traditional organisations successfully introduced strong hierarchies, rigid rules and made work increasingly specialised. That's why we are now used to shaping our organisations like pyramids - with inflexible departments separated by layers of management. Most of us have fixed job functions and our responsibilities are strictly defined. Once, this approach made sense, provided a successful formula for many companies and dominated large areas of the 20th century business environment. Taylor's legacy forces the greater number of employees to deal with work that is simply not fun - and this is because the workplace he designed for the 20th century no longer fits. It often makes it harder to get work done. Decision making is incredibly slow, collaboration and communication frustrated by politics, and on Wednesdays we celebrate the week having reached its mid-point. Our desires to take the initiative or innovate are discouraged. It seems that the world of management thinking is becoming a collection of dead ideas.

We quit
our jobs in a
quest to make
our working
lives
— and yours —
more fun.

We quit our jobs in a quest to make our working lives — and yours — more fun. That's why we started Corporate Rebels, drafted our Bucket List, and set out to meet our heroes. Remember — there was no checklist for pioneers, no criteria to be ticked off. We reasoned that they all could teach us something about making work more fun. We didn't just search for progressive corporates, we sought out entrepreneurs, gurus, writers, academics and experts of every stripe. Our list soon outgrew the Catalan beer mat, and within days included 100 items. These were not only household names; we didn't want a list that consisted entirely of famous people. Nor did we want a list solely of young tech companies or modern, hip, start-ups. We wanted as much diversity as possible: to invalidate stereotypes and prove once and for all that work – any work – can be fun. Regardless of the job, and where it's performed; even in places where you would least expect it, such as government organisations, or whitegoods manufacturers in China.

We hunted for progressive organisations of all sizes. Some were multinationals, others were small but perfectly formed – from deep in the Dutch polder to the other side of the planet. We investigated many interesting sectors including manufacturing, government, and a bank with thousands of employees. Even an American submarine. Our Bucket List is graced with inspiring companies found in the most unlikely places – and that is sometimes part of their strength. It's direct evidence that you can make work enjoyable and rewarding, even in the most challenging environments. It is possible in every company, and can be applied in every industry, everywhere in the world. It was time to start ticking off these names, but before we begin our story, here's a thought we would like to share. This book does not pretend to be a ready-made solution, a magic spell to turn your workplace into paradise. These ideas are inspiration for change. Take from it what you need. This book is an overture to options, ideas, and inspiration, not a doctrine to follow. What you make of it is up to you and we hope you enjoy the journey.

BUCKET LIST

Our Bucket List is comprised of pioneers, rebels, revolutionaries, academics, employees, employers and business leaders. People who change the face of frustrating workplaces and bring joy to the job.

We check off our Bucket List by visiting these individuals and organisations. We learn from them and share their insights. Check out the full and most recent list at corporate-rebels.com/bucketlist. Click on the names and read our findings.

170 PIONEERS

Aaron Dignan
Abdulla Al Karam
Adam Grant
Alexander Kjerulf
Amy Edmondson
Anja van der Horst
Ari Weinzweig
Arnaud Collery
Atlassian
August
Bakker van Maanen
Barry Lutgens
Basecamp
Beetroot
Ben Kuiken
Bill Fischer
Bjarte Bogsnes
Bob Hutten
Bol.com
Breman

Brewdog
Bruggink van der Velden
Bunnik Plants
Bushe
Buurtzorg
Carin Wormsbecher
Carlos Saba
Centigo
Charlie Kim
Clipper Bro
Chris Rufer
Chris White
Christobal Colon
Chuck Blakeman
Clovis Bojikian
Cyberclick
Dan Price
Daniel Pink
Daniel Urban
Darren Childs
David Burkus
David Heinemeier Hansson
David Marquet
David Tomas
Dee Hock

Dennis Bakke

~~Dominic Jackman~~

~~Doug Kirkpatrick~~

~~Edalco~~

Eddie Obeng

Emmanuele Duez

~~Enspiral~~

~~Familiehulp~~

~~Finext~~

~~Fons Trompenaars~~

~~FPS Social Security~~

Francesca Gino

~~Frank van Massenhove~~

~~Frederic Laloux~~

~~Freitag~~

Futurice

Garry Ridge

Gary Hamel

~~Good Rebels~~

Goodwood

~~Google~~

Gravity Payments

~~Haier~~

Hamdi Ulukaya

Handelsbanken

Happy

~~Harm Jans~~

~~Haufe Umantis~~

HCL Technologies

Helen Bevan

Henry Mintzberg

~~Henry Stewart~~

~~H-Farm~~

Hollands Kroon

Hoppenbrouwers

Hutten

~~IDEO~~

Incentro

~~Isaac Getz~~

~~Jaap Peters~~

Jack Hubbard

Jack Stack

Jaipur Rugs

James Watt

Jason Fried

~~Jason Trost~~

~~Jean Francois Zobrist~~

Jean Oelwang

~~Jens Wiklund~~

John Lewis

~~Jos De Blok~~

~~Julian Birkinshaw~~

~~K2K Emocionando~~

~~Katarina Berg~~

~~Kath Blackham~~

~~Kees Pater~~

~~Ken Everett~~

~~KHDA Dubai~~

~~Koekjesbakkerij~~

~~Veldt~~

~~Koldo Saratxaga~~

La Fageda

~~Lars Kolind~~

Laszlo Bock

~~Marc Stoffel~~

Mario Kaplan

~~Mark Vletter~~

Massimo Bottura

~~Mathieu Weggeman~~

~~Matt Black Systems~~

Matt Perez

Megan Reitz

~~Meghan Messenger~~

~~Meike Bartels~~

~~Menlo Innovations~~

Mike Arauz

Mindbox

~~Morning Star~~

Nand Kishore Chaudhary

~~Nearsoft~~

Netflix

~~Next Jump~~

~~Nikki Gatenby~~

~~Niverplast~~

Patagonia

Patty McCord

~~Paul Green Jr.~~

~~Propellernet~~

Qiwi

~~Rebel Group~~

~~Remmelt Schuuring~~

~~Rene van Loon~~

~~Ricardo Semler~~

Richard Branson

~~Richard Nieuwenhuis~~

~~Richard Sheridan~~

~~Rosabeth Moss Kanter~~

Rose Marcario

~~Schoenen Torfs~~

~~SchoonGewoon~~

~~Semco~~	~~Voys~~
SEMrush	W.L. Gore
Sharmadean Reid	~~WCLC~~
~~Simon Sinek~~	WD40
~~Sjoerd van der Velden~~	Wedding
~~Smarkets~~	~~Wouter Torfs~~
Sol	~~WP Haton~~
~~Spotify~~	Xavier Huillard
Stanley McCrystal	~~Yuri van Geest~~
~~The Ready~~	Yves Morieux
~~TMC~~	Yvon Chouinard
~~Tom Peters~~	~~Zappos~~
~~Tom van der Lubbe~~	~~Zhang Ruimin~~
~~Tony's Chocolonely~~	~~Zingerman's~~
~~Traci Fenton~~	
~~U2i~~	
~~UKTV~~	
Upstalsboom	
~~Vagas~~	
Valve	
~~Versa~~	
~~Viisi~~	
Vineet Nayar	
Virgin	
Vkusvill	

CHAPTER 1

FROM PROFIT TO PURPOSE & VALUES

It is pitch black in the campervan. We know it well enough to find things in the dark; we have been travelling through California for the past month, but this is our last week in the United States. Highway 1 has been our home for three weeks, a magnificent, meandering coastal road that runs from Los Angeles to San Francisco. The alarm was set to go off early, because today we have Rebel business. We roll up our sleeping bags and fold our beds with a sense of purpose. The beach of Ventura, remember? Soon we're standing on the chilly sands, watching the dolphins and surfers and waiting for our first pioneer of good people management: Chipper Bro, one of Patagonia's first employees.

Patagonia is an American retail company founded in 1973 by fanatical mountaineer Yvon Chouinard. A lack of specialised gear in the day forced him to make his own equipment. He taught himself to forge iron, that's how serious he was. And the gear he produced wasn't make-do, home-made junk. It soon became so popular with the climbing community that he decided to make this his living. Slowly, the company he formed grew into a worldwide player. It has diversified over the years, and today Patagonia is not solely focused on climbers; it makes equipment for skiers, snowboarders, surfers, fly-fishers, and runners. None of these sports requires an engine, you might notice; these are activities that prioritise a bond between athlete and nature. Unsurprising, then, that the Patagonia headquarters are sequestered in this idyllic part of the Californian coast.

We wander along the beach, relishing the morning's beauty but wondering where the hell Chipper Bro is. We explore in the half-light, but before we get very far Chipper Bro arrives in a white van. He sticks his head out: "Dudes, you ready for some surf today? Rad!" Patagonia's Chipper Bro, officially known as Chip Bell, is an 11-time World Frisbee Freestyle champion. With his wild mane of grey curls, Chipper looks just like a hippie. He gets out of the van and envelops us both in the sort of hugs you come to expect from free spirits in southern California. Soon he has us laughing, and after a quick introduction opens the back of his van. It's full of surfing gear. Chipper rummages around and conjures up two black wetsuits that fit us surprisingly well. Naturally enough, it's Patagonia's brand. Another scuffle in the van and out he pops again, this time with two surfboards. Chipper thrusts the boards at us and leads the way. "Before we talk about Patagonia," he calls over his shoulder, "I want to have you guys experience what we're all about." It's still chilly, and we do some exercises to warm our muscles.

A surfing session is a fitting introduction and wholly in keeping with the corporate philosophy of its founder. The title of Yvon Chouinard's autobiography speaks volumes: *Let My People Go Surfing: The Education of a Reluctant Businessman.* For the next hour we make clumsy attempts to find our balance as the grey waves hurl us toward the shore. It's harder than it looks. Chipper takes wave after wave. We try to kid ourselves that we aren't doing too badly, and by the end of the session we manage to stand for a second or two. After we have taken enough of a battering, we call it a day. Exhausted but satisfied we flop down on the sand; behind us the sun deigns at last to show its face. Sitting cross-legged on the beach, Chipper looks out across the ocean and says: "I'm just super-stoked you guys are here. I want to properly acquaint you with our organisation, so let's go to the office. There's a decent breakfast waiting for us there." We stow the wetsuits and surfboards, and within minutes we're at Patagonia HQ. It's not your usual company base, a rambling agglomeration of compact, colourful buildings that house about 600 staff members. We notice some campervans in the parking lot, and several cars draped with wetsuits, hanging out to dry. A very special corporate headquarters indeed!

How we spend our days is, of course, how we spend our lives.

Annie Dillard

As Pulitzer Prize-winning writer Annie Dillard puts it: "How we spend our days is, of course, how we spend our lives." The work we do says a lot about the way we lead our lives. Imagine this: you're 80 years old and surrounded by your grandkids. They ask you about the things you are most proud of. You reflect on your life, and poke about in your past. Filled with pride, you tell them about the life you lived... Would you mention your job or the meaningful work you did with your colleagues? Did your career contribute to a better world? Research at the University of Leiden concludes that 25 percent[7] of employees doubt the usefulness of their work. In his book *Bullshit Jobs*[8], anthropologist David Graeber quotes a British study showing that 37 percent of workers feel that their job does not make a useful contribution to society.

Of course, meaningful work is not always an option, especially when people are struggling just to survive. But in the western world, this is not usually the case. Why do we accept that work is just about making money? Why do we agree to work for a boss whose only goal is to get richer, and for shareholders who don't look beyond the next quarter? These narrow-minded aspirations do not sit well with modern thinking, and result in unhappy employees. What if, instead of accepting this sort of situation, we spent our time on work that has a positive impact? How nice it would be to work for organisations that believe in positive change. We felt for ourselves the painful mismatch between the work we did for large corporations and our personal desire to feel useful. Decisions were largely based on profit. The entire strategy was about money; the only measure of success, financial. Focusing on maximising profits promotes morbid short-term thinking. Managers are pushed by stakeholders to take decisions that ensure a swift return on investment, often at the expense of everything and everyone. This is not good for the world and is demotivating. A recent paper in *The Journal of Business Ethics*[9], backed-up by five studies, showed employee motivation is 17 to 33 percent higher when profit is not the primary concern. This is old news; for decades research has shown that the pursuit of a higher purpose motivates more strongly than pursuit of a higher profit. When we visited Bucket List pioneer and bestselling author Daniel Pink (*Drive: The Surprising Truth about What Motivates Us*), we learned more. "The question, 'What difference do I make in the world?' is essential," he said. "Being aware of your contribution is extremely motivating. The paradox is that many organisations do nothing when it comes to creating a higher purpose.

"There is a big difference between what science knows and what happens in real life. Even organisations aware of the issue commit another grave mistake: they assume their employees and customers are not that bright. This is how it goes: A leader wakes up, and thinks "Yes, we need to move with the times." A decision is made to follow the 'purpose hype'. They hire consultants to decide on their noble goal, without involving their employees. The result? A goal. Wonderful. Now what? Purpose-setting will not by itself have the desired effect. At worst, it's lipstick on a pig: a sham that demotivates employees even more. How about a campaign to let the world know how purpose-driven the organisation is? The result is a feel-good TV commercial and a catchy jingle; nothing changes. Decisions are still based on the same motivation; managers are promoted and rewarded according to the short-term profits, and projects are assessed on financial value. For the employees, who were never involved in the first place, nothing changes.

The question,
'What difference
do I make in the
world?' is essential.
Being aware of your
contribution is
extremely motivating.
The paradox is that
many organisations do
nothing when it
comes to creating
a higher purpose.

— Daniel Pink

CALIFORNIA STYLE

The vibe we find at Patagonia somehow reminds us of a mountain cabin. Chipper's desk is near the entrance. He is Patagonia's receptionist, among other things – the first person many visitors see. Employees arrive in dribs and drabs while Chipper leads us to the shared breakfast space. The atmosphere is relaxed, there is murmured conversation and laughter. This is the way to start the day. Some are accompanied by children, others by pets. Now this is the informal workplace we knew existed and have been seeking...

After breakfast we take a seat at the wooden picnic table in the now balmy California sunshine. Over the course of the day, a steady flow of employees comes to visit. People share their stories and answer our barrage of questions. There is no typical worker, or age bracket; we speak to all sorts. There are social media experts, distribution employees, interns, members of management. Everyone seems to share the same passions: outdoor life, adrenaline sports, fitness, nature. At Patagonia, everything is about that higher purpose. It is embodied in their expressions and attitudes. This is a free-thinking collection of rambling, intelligent, unusual, interesting people, not drones. They really believe in what they make – and use the products in their free-time passions. The bond with nature creates something of a fellowship – but there is devotion too for the organisation. The authenticity and engagement of Patagonia's employees is evident, and inspiring. It is something not often seen in a workplace. "We want to set the standard for others to follow," one employee told us, "but in the end, we want to do what's right." That's wonderful to hear, but how does it work in the real world?

A wooden plaque, engraved with the Patagonia mission statement, hangs above Chipper's desk. *"Build the best products, cause no unnecessary harm, use business to inspire and implement solutions*

34

to the environmental crisis," it reads. Take the first part: *build the best product.* This is Patagonia's raison d'être. The company pushes itself to provide the very best. Founder Chouinard wrote in his autobiography: "We are a product-driven business, and without this there can't be a company. Useful products of good quality represent our anchor."[10] This attitude inspires employees on many levels. Whatever task is being undertaken – setting-up social media channels, providing customer service, researching and delivering studies, outfitting retail stores, running the childcare service – it is done with maximum care. It's the best. Childcare service, we hear you ask? Certainly. Our table is surrounded by children happily playing while their parents work. And every now and again, an employee will take a few minutes out to come and play with the kids. This childcare service captures the essence of our search in many ways; we ask Chipper Bro about it. It was a pragmatic solution, he explains. "During the first years, many of us were at an age to start a family. Some employees – including Yvon and his wife Malinda – started bringing their kids to work. It wasn't long before the first cribs appeared. Naturally, this wasn't thrilling for everyone. Crying kids aren't what you want at your place of work, after all. It took another two years before the solution presented itself. We hire an expert and start our own childcare service."

Here, too, Patagonia is a pioneer, working with new legislation. The service is led by qualified teachers. Children are encouraged to learn from nature and spend as much time as possible outdoors. This service is great for the staff, and the company benefits. "After maternity leave 95 percent of (Patagonia) employees return to work," one of the mothers tells us, "compared to a national average of 64 percent. Half our managers and senior leadership team members are women." It becomes apparent that this return rate saves Patagonia $350,000 per annum[11] — the amount it would cost to attract, interview and employ new workers. Good for people, good for business. And there

Patagonia people have a uniting sense of purpose. This minimises the need for rules and regulations.
The credo acts as a guideline for every project.

is more to the higher purpose: *cause no unnecessary harm, use business to inspire and implement solutions to the environmental crisis.* Patagonia considers the impact of its production process and has done so for years. Its soul-searching pulls no punches, and sometimes has serious consequences for the core business. An employee who has been with Patagonia from the start tells us all about it. "From the early '80s, we started to look at our role as polluter. For example, our product catalogue. The paper version was an important sales item. We sent it everywhere.

"But it was printed on ordinary paper and this was no longer acceptable. We decided in 1990 that we would use only recycled material, found only one acceptable alternative, and it was still very much in the testing phase. It would mean cutting back on print quality. The pictures became vague, the colours bland. But 14,500 trees were saved, so it was worth the effort. The following year, the reproduction improved and soon the recycled paper matched our old standard."

Dedication to that higher purpose provides a clear direction. It ensures that the company can take decisions that benefit it and the planet. During the '90s, the company once again looked at its supply chain with a critical eye. Patagonia investigated the polluting characteristics of the fibres that it used most: wool, polyester, nylon and cotton. The researchers found that the cultivation of conventional cotton is highly polluting, uses a lot of chemicals that poison the earth, air, and groundwater. Cotton is also a thirsty plant, a drain on precious water resources. In 1994, Patagonia took the bold decision to ban the use of conventional material and replace it with organically grown cotton where possible. Once again, Patagonia was a pioneer.

It was a risky undertaking, with some serious consequences. At the time, 20 percent of Patagonia's revenue came from products made with conventionally grown cotton. The cultivation of the organic alternative was still in its infancy. Patagonia felt an obligation to act and set up a whole new industry, with $20 million in revenue at stake. The company succeeded in getting its work family behind this resolution. Excursions to local cotton fields were arranged. "We saw the environmental damage caused by the cultivation of cotton and use of pesticides," an employee told us. "We could experience the benefits. Hundreds of us went on these excursions, and most decided to buy organic products from that moment on. The organisation supported the decision." Money was put where mouths are and within two years, the job was done. Patagonia uses almost entirely organic cotton, accepting a three-fold cost increase. That meant fewer kinds of available fabric – and a cut in the range from 91 styles to 66.

That higher purpose –recently updated to "We're in business to save our home planet" –is deeply rooted. "We vet our partners and work only with organisations that act in a sustainable and responsible manner. But sure, we will never be 100 percent content. Improvement and sustainability are constant challenges. It's not just about making clothes or printing catalogues." Patagonia people have a uniting sense of purpose. This minimises the need for rules and regulations. The credo acts as a guideline for every project. It improves efficiency and communication, as well as autonomy. No one's waiting for orders from the boss before acting.

A younger employee tells us about the Patagonia way of creating new office space. "Our preference is to find an old building that we can save from demolition. Failing that, we'll build – but for refurb and decoration we use only recycled materials. This is the most responsible way to go, and it's a good fit with our philosophy." Our visit coincides with election time, and the Patagonia people are getting involved. "Vote Our Planet" is their campaign motto, set up by employees but embraced by all. The goal is to motivate Americans and nudge them in the right direction. Patagonia has made $1 million available to support candidates that advocate clean water, clean air and sustainable energy." After our visit, the company closes for the day. "We want to encourage employees and customers to vote," Chipper explains. Not much later we hear his voice boom over the intercom: "Ladies and gentlemen. Good morning, I wish all a wonderful day. Tomorrow is important, and I am asking you for a small favour: Don't forget to vote! Every single one will count."

Not long after, Patagonia once again walks the walk. It donates the profits of its 2016 Black Friday sales — a record $10 million — to environmental groups. Every cent of it. By doing so, it supported hundreds of non-profits; this sort of action makes Patagonia more than a brand. It's a societal advisor for the change it wants to see, to make a difference and influence consumer choices and responsibilities. This is something we will see often in our travels. Progressives start revolutions, they don't just make money. They crusade.

CHOCOLATE AND BEETROOT

We visited the head office of online shoe store Zappos in Las Vegas, where everything is designed to "deliver happiness". We found an even more powerful example in Amsterdam, where confectioner Tony's Chocolonely works to eliminate the slave trade that has plagued the cocoa industry and made chocolate an increasingly guilty pleasure. And then there is the mortgage lender Viisi, working to create a sustainable future for the financial world. Or the Swedish-Ukrainian company Beetroot, that works to raise living standards in rural Ukraine by providing education and employment. These progressives embrace higher purpose, and ensure the focus is never solely on profit margins. A fixation with finances can lead to failure, but revolutions never die.

Every action should be linked to an ethical outcome, these companies believe, and employees empathise with that caring attitude. They feel closer to their employers as a result. An inspiring purpose gives a sense of belonging, and people generally want to be part of a community. They want to be part of change, part of a revolution. Part of something that has meaning. Profit is important, of course. It funds the pursuit of purpose, but should be the means, not the end. Profit for a company is like oxygen for a human: necessary to stay alive, but not the reason for living.

A higher purpose defines the goal. It doesn't say how it should be reached, or how people should interact. It doesn't need to be protected by rules, procedures and protocols. Core values provide direction and motivation. Only a few of the world's corporations have values that are adhered to and used as a driving force. Values should be entrenched in all activities: recruitment, selection, rewards, on-boarding, decision-making, leave of absence, holidays. Initiatives should follow this flow. Eliminating rules without setting up clear principles to take their place is irresponsible. This is an exercise that must be more than company propaganda. It's about authenticity.

Deep within the Dutch polder, there is a town council that shows the power of an inspiring higher purpose. Intrigued by what we have heard, we get back on the road to visit the rebels Anja van der Horst and Wim van Twuijver. They are directors of the Hollands Kroon Council, a fusion of towns in the north. On our way, we see a Dutch landscape so typical it could be a postcard scene: a polder, complete with canals and windmills. At the council offices, Van der Horst leads us to a pleasant workspace. The lighting looks somehow festive. This director of business operations is a woman with an inviting smile and easy-going manner. With short, curly hair and a black leather jacket she has that rebel look. She offers coffee and we take a seat. As one of the three directors, Anja van der Horst has been spearheading a remarkable transformation of the council. "The new municipality started in 2012, in North-Holland (one of the 12 counties, or provinces, in the Netherlands). Hollands Kroon comprises the towns Anna Paulowna, Wieringen, Wieringermeer, and Niedorp. A group of mayors and aldermen had been working towards change. "What are we achieving?" they asked themselves. "What is our added value? What do we want to mean to the public?"

Hollands Kroon determined to become the smartest municipality in the Netherlands in response to an ever-changing world. "People ask for speed, efficiency, and customisation," says Van der Horst. "That means that local governments have to break through old patterns. Can things be done better, cheaper, and more easily?" The power of core values comes from taking strategic steps towards improvement, and that's what Hollands Kroon did. It considered six core values: trust, grit, enthusiasm, contact, respect, and innovation, and imple-

We ended
up ditching
70 percent
of the rules

— Anja van der Horst

mented them, with input from all employees. "It is a gradual process. The values are not a purpose – they are part of our identity."

Trust comes first; it ensures that unnecessary rules can be safely abolished. There is no need to ask permission for leave, or to verify working hours. Employees have a say in how education and development budgets are spent. The power of choice is put into the hands of the workers. Customer service was revitalised, and the municipal code had a shake-up. "We ended up ditching 70 percent of the rules," says Van der Horst. "I believe that showing trust brings many good things." Co-operation is the norm for Hollands Kroon residents. There is a focus on resolving problems digitally, or remotely. Questions are answered via the website, social media, or by phone. If help is still required, the civil servant will visit the person in question to nut-out a solution. Products and services are often free-of-charge. Hollands Kroon is the first Dutch municipality to deliver passports at no cost, six days a week, anywhere in the Netherlands. This is the council that will come to you.

There were unavoidable redundancies, and this is where the core value of Respect came in. "Some left by choice, but others were let go," Van der Horst explains. "We treated everyone with respect, and they all left us as ambassadors. No legal proceedings were necessary." Those joining must sit the core values test. "This helps them to decide whether Hollands Kroon will suit them. It is also where all potential new colleagues get the chance to properly 'meet' Holland Kroon. CVs do not matter, personalities do. Only when there is a good fit will a candidate go through to the next round when skills become a consideration. There are often two or three selection stages, each with different criteria. Sometimes it is a case study, sometimes role-playing, and sometimes a trial working day. There are many possibilities."

We saw similar principles at work at music streaming service Spotify, which abides by the motto: "Hire for culture, train for skills". Of the 100 people it recruits each month, attention is first given to a match for cultural fit. Only later will there be a focus on talents, qualifications and skills. HR director Katarina Berg enlightened us when we visited the head office in Stockholm. "First we did it the other way around," she said. "That made it difficult to not hire someone who had excellent skills but did not match our core values. So, we do the cultural interview first. This little change really helped strengthen us."

At Hollands Kroon, more radical steps have been taken, and the results are remarkable. Managers and departments have been arranged into a structure of three directors and 35 self-managing teams of on average five to eight people. These teams have responsibility for their budgets, recruitment, communications, and make themselves available to residents. Private offices have been abolished, along with the "clock-in" mentality. Rather rebellious steps for an organisation with 330 employees. Especially a government one.

PIONEERING PRACTICES FROM AROUND THE GLOBE

Higher corporate purposes and core values may sound airy-fairy, but once you consider the potential benefits you may come to view them as imperative. Our Bucket List pioneers have proved that purpose pays off. It improves staff motivation and involvement and is directly linked to better financial results. Companies with a focus on a higher purpose perform up to 10 times better than the competition[12]. Consumers are willing to pay more for products and services from companies that focus on having a positive influence[13].

In the Harvard Business Review, Professor Adam Grant and colleagues discuss what an organisation should do to attract and retain talent[14]. Their unsurprising findings: higher purpose and decent core values are strong motivators. How do you ensure that the purpose and values of an organisation become central? What have these 100-plus visits to pioneers shown us? What differentiates progressives? Here are some rebellious ways to make your organisation stand up and stand out.

LEVEL 1. HAVE A BOLD PURPOSE

Go in head-first! Then reach out to like-minded souls in companies, charities, suppliers, and your customers and employees. Encourage them to join the revolution – or at least contribute to yours. The purpose must tick boxes: it must be authentic, honest, fearless and real. It is a corporate moral compass, helping to set a steady course in good times and bad. The higher purpose must provide a true sense of direction – especially in times of frustration or loss. No matter how confusing or challenging things become, your purpose is your rock. The most powerful examples provide answers to questions such as: Why does our company exist? Why do we do what we do? What is our added value? Who are we? Do we mean what we say? Who are we doing this for? What difference do we want to make? The answers must form guidelines for every action, every decision, every person.

LEVEL 2. GET THE MESSAGE TO EVERYONE

The higher purpose must be shared. Whether it's your first day with the organisation or your last, whether you're the boss or not, the purpose doesn't change. Think back to Patagonia and the trips to the cotton fields. Consider the example set by Zappos, where all employees work in customer service before taking on other roles. These people get experience that helps them understand why things are done the way they are.

The higher purpose and core values must be applied in all areas. Make sure that every department, every team, every person is aware of their contribution.

LEVEL 3. HIRE FOR CULTURE, TRAIN FOR SKILLS

The founder of Southwest Airlines, Herb Kelleher, once said: "The business of business is people." Southwest hires for values. It understands that employees are the custodians of corporate culture. It pays to be ruthless in this area. You can train people to fly planes and serve passengers; but you can't change who they are. That is why this airline works hard on attentive hiring that filters or redirects those unsuited to their roles within a six-month probationary period. A survey of employees showed 75 percent saw their job as "a calling", and 86 percent were proud to work for the airline[15]. Isn't that what it's all about?

LEVEL 4. MEASURE IMPACT, TRACK PROGRESS, SHARE IT WIDELY

Are you accomplishing your goals? Employees need to see their own role as part of the bigger picture. Knowing that your actions contribute to the greater good provides immense satisfaction. Measure, and be transparent, authentic and honest. Every year, Patagonia reveals its pollution rates and those of the non-profits it supports. Tony's Chocolonely measures how slavery develops within the cocoa industry, and honestly and openly communicates that information.

LEVEL 5. PUT YOUR MONEY WHERE YOUR MOUTH IS

It doesn't matter how loud your voice is, your actions are all-important. Authenticity and credibility are lost when you fail to follow through. Patagonia halted profitable lines to cut pollution and donated its Black Friday profits to worthy causes. It also directs one percent of its annual revenue to non-profits. Every day it stands by its higher purpose.

CHAPTER 2

FROM HIERARCHICAL PYRAMID TO NETWORK OF TEAMS

Since 2016, we have visited our fair share of CEOs, entrepreneurs, academics, and gurus and getting a foot in the door isn't always easy. We have honed our stalking skills and scored some wonderful meetings. We are nonetheless struggling to wangle an invitation to one of our Bucket List companies: Chinese whitegoods and electronics manufacturer Haier. We try many times to contact CEO Zhang Ruimin, without success. Our luck changes after the umpteenth email, another phone call, and a few favours. We receive an invitation to Qingdao, and the head office of Haier.

We can't wait to look behind the scenes. One month later, we find ourselves on a plane heading east. It's late evening when we arrive at Qingdao, where two Haier employees are waiting. They give us a brief introduction while the minibus driver navigates the chaotic Chinese traffic. They reveal the schedule for the coming week, an imposing document that resembles the itinerary for an international trade mission. Each day is planned, with visits to factories and the Haier museum, as well as meetings with employees. The highlight, of course, will be the conversation with Zhang Ruimin.

It's the week before Christmas, and we spend a few days in Qingdao, a coastal city, to form a picture of the organisation's home turf, to study our prey in its natural environment, so to speak. We're jetlagged, but there's no time for leisurely acclimatisation. The driver is at our door bright and early to ferry us to the HQ. We are not alone. In honour of our visit, Haier has arranged for a translator and jour- nalist to fly over from Shanghai. And that's not all. A short time after, a camera crew from Haier's in-house TV-channel will appear. The Haier people are keen to share, but that works both ways; they want to hear what we've gleaned from others. We're good with that, but for us this is the time to finally unpick Haier's secrets. This means a lot to us. We've been wondering how a production giant with a workforce the size of a modest regional centre can function – and reinvent itself. We want it from the horse's mouth, and that means time with Zhang Ruimin, Haier's enigmatic chief executive.

Zhang is a friendly 70-year-old, wise and well versed in the ways of business. He has studied management history and is given to quoting some of the gurus we too admire. Every other minute he references Peter Drucker and Gary Hamel. Ruimin deserves to be quoted himself, and somewhere outside this office, that is doubtless happen- ing. But Ruimin is a humble man, despite the apparent magic required to turn Haier from a small, almost bankrupt operation into the largest manufacturer of household appliances in the world. The process has taken four decades.

It is therefore not entirely surprising when, during one of our later visits, we run into Gary Hamel. This American professor and best-selling author has been fighting the paralyzing, organisational ailment of bureaucracy for years. Despite Hamel's battle, there is very little real change. His study shows that larger businesses are tending to become more conservative and still feature eight or more levels of management. Eight! And each of these layers usually has something to say about the work being done by the people lower down the pyramid.

"Bureaucracy is increasing," Hamel tells us. But why? Organisations are creating rules, and centralising. That costs money. A lot of money. According to the study that Hamel and his colleague Michele Zanini carried out, the effects of bureaucracy cost society, in the US alone, some $3 trillion every year. The structure is an ugly spike with the board of directors at the top, and below that, layer by layer, levels of management. At the bottom of this stifling heap are the people who carry out the real work. This is a recipe for disaster, and communication between departments is flawed because everyone defends their own little fiefdom. That's understandable; after all, each department is judged on its performance. Sales makes a deal and tosses it to Production. Production tries to run with the ball, but by doing so clashes with Marketing. Marketing has its own battle with Finance, and Finance fights everyone. This cold warfare often takes precedence over the effort to please the client, which does nobody any favours. Traditional structures worry 92 percent of organisation heads[15], according to studies, who see it as the highest priority – and rightly so. But despite apparent awareness, in practice there are issues to overcome. Of those leaders canvassed, 86 percent are pulling their hair out because they don't know how to tackle the issue [15].

What do you do
with 76 broken
fridges?
I called for my
employees to join
me, took a
sledgehammer, and
smashed one of
them to pieces.

– Zhang Ruimin

There is a big difference between recognising a need for change and making it happen. Instead of providing regular updates, many companies keep plugging away at what they know best. Dubious practices follow, such as endless co-ordination-and-update meetings. Research from the University of Nebraska shows that up to 55 million meetings take place in the US every day[16], and the average employee spends six hours of the week in one of them. It's even worse for managers, who, on average, spend about 23 hours in meetings each week. And at least half of those hours are eventually deemed "unproductive", aka a waste of time and money. The painful consequence, according to the researchers, is that organisations "waste $213 billion (equivalent to California's fiscal spending plans for 2019) on bad meetings that, very often, only make things worse".

(HINESE WHISPERS

At Haier, we know that Zhang Ruimin can tell us all about bureaucratic messes. But there is one problem: he does not speak English and we don't speak Mandarin or Cantonese. A convoluted process is put in motion. The first stage is a room with leather chairs and an oversized hardwood table: your average meeting room, with space for at least 20. Microphones are evenly spaced; Corporate Rebels sit on one side, Zhang and his entourage on the other. We pose questions via the translator. Also in the room is a camera crew recording each detail, a couple of photographers clicking away, and a small army of others whose function is unclear. Despite the language barrier, the conversation flows smoothly. Zhang explains the path, and the challenges, of the transformation process.

Changes are seldom permanent, and few last as long as a decade. Zhang takes us on the journey of Haier's five major transformations. It is an instructive lesson in successful management. "In 1984, I was appointed head of the local refrigerator factory by the council of Qingdao," Zhang recalls. "It was a gamble on their part, but the factory had been making losses for ages. It became my job to make something of this chaos." That was no mean feat, because years of shoddy management meant that the factory had heavy debt, the workshop was a mess, and almost no one was working — because there simply wasn't much to do.

"We received a letter from an angry customer. Her newly purchased fridge was already broken. This was an unpleasant surprise and I checked the factory stock. I was speechless. Twenty percent of all the fridges the company had manufactured — 76 in total — were faulty. This was unacceptable. But what do you do with 76 broken fridges? On impulse, I had them all put on display in the middle of the factory floor. I called for my employees to join me, took a sledgehammer, and smashed one of them to pieces. Not the most civilised action but it did have the desired effect. Fridges were insanely expensive at the time, on average two full-year salaries for a factory worker. My staff stood and watched, horrified.

"After I had finished smashing that first fridge, I invited them to do the same with the rest." This dramatic deed was the beginning of a decades-long transformation. After the orgy of destruction, Zhang called a meeting. It was the starting point for the first major transformation. "I desperately wanted order. China does not have much of a management history to draw upon, so I didn't know where to begin. I started delving into Western and Eastern management ideas. Looking to the West, I saw that many companies in America and Europe organised themselves in hierarchical pyramids. Japanese companies were experimenting with principles such as Lean and Total Quality Management.

"That inspired us to organise the factory as a pyramid and focus on constant improvement and innovation." Haier soon became a respected name in the Chinese market. It came to be synonymous with high-quality products and awards followed. After Haier had made its name at home, global recognition became the goal. Zhang knew that to keep growing, he would have to produce a range of products. During the 1990s, the decision was made to buy out loss-making factories. Zhang used an unusual strategy here. Haier acquired only factories that ticked two boxes: a good product... and bad management.

By changing the management style of these factories, Haier swiftly turned them to profit, without putting in a lot of money. Zhang learned how important it is to listen to employees. "As long as the staff are prepared to use their talents, management is successful. In the '90s, our main goal was to build a world-famous brand. We had to give employees space to contribute." Ironically, or tellingly, it was the rapid growth of the 1990s that highlighted the limitations of the hierarchical pyramid. Haier's progress slowed and performance took a dive. It was time to regroup. "When we realised that we had to replace the pyramid," says Zhang, "I once again looked to global management styles. In the West I saw the rise of the matrix model. Employees were divided into teams based on function, reporting to superiors and project leaders. This form of multi-headed control turned out to be exactly what we needed."

During this second transformation, Haier was reborn in the matrix mould. Along with this came initiatives to stimulate innovation. Employees who came up with the most effective proposals to improve matters or solve a pernicious problem were rewarded — and had the honour of having their innovations named after them. During our visit to one of Haier's factories, we witnessed this. An employee told us about a process that was named after him, and he gained a lot of respect from colleagues. This led to constant brainwaves, with employees driven to spend their own time developing projects and ideas. A period of expansion ensued — growth so rapid that in the closing years of the decade, Haier became China's largest fridge manufacturer. The success led to exports – under its own, once unpopular, name. This was unusual in China, where products are generally manufactured under licence for Western brands. Zhang's faith in his staff and products was a vote of confidence in the organisation.

The daring tactic quickly paid off. Haier had made its mark in developing and established markets, locally and internationally. After the turn of the millennium, Haier had a brand that was not only recognised, but admired. But in business, things never seem to run smoothly for very long. Things at Haier started to go awry once more. Staff began to find limitations in the matrix. Production slowed, frustration set in, internal systems seemed to be losing efficiency. People were spending more time writing reports than working for clients.

"The pyramid worked really well during the 1980s and the matrix was excellent in the '90s," Zhang told us, "but early in the millennium we grew so much that the system couldn't keep up." It was again time

The head office culture was dismantled.
The process was hindered and complicated by those in power, who were reluctant to release their death grip on the tiller.

for transformation, but by now change — once feared and avoided — had become an anticipated part of continued progress and even welcomed. Zhang saw that multinationals were experimenting with satellite organisations. In the early 2000s, he decided to follow suit. With the breathtaking rise of the internet, the fourth transformation came sooner than Haier had anticipated. The world wide web allowed clients to compare products and services, and consequently demand that their specific needs be met. Haier decided to match supply to demand, and to deliver products only when the market was ready. Zhang took the bold step of working without stock and producing to order. That's risky, because you don't want to keep customers waiting. To minimise delivery time, Haier began increasing local production by buying-out foreign brands. In Japan, it acquired the household appliance department of Sanyo; in New Zealand, Fisher & Pakel was scooped-up. In America, Haier went for a household name — General Electric — and completed a partial buy-out.

Still seated at the oversized Haier conference table, Zhang continues: "We also worked hard to change things internally. We were starting to feel the bottleneck while trying to please clients. We knew that it was time for another change. Wherever I looked, I saw only pyramids, matrices, and satellite organisations. I couldn't find evidence of any other major innovations and didn't find much inspiration. This was the moment we became pioneers."

THINKING LIKE ENTREPRENEURS

Zhang threw the traditional structure out the window, dividing the company into 2,000 Zi Zhu Jing Ying Ti's (ZZJYTs). These are self-organising units, moving away from hierarchical pyramids towards team networks. These ZZJYT teams provide employees with the freedom to keep innovating and thinking like entrepreneurs. In this structure, everyone could propose a new product or service. Workers, suppliers and customers decided by vote which proposals had the most potential, and these were used to create new ZZJYT units. The person who came up with the idea was appointed leader. He or she would then gather a team, and all other employees could join the ZZJYT if they thought they would be able to add value. From this point, rewards were based on performance. The teams now strongly resembled small autonomous companies.

Haier is ever evolving, and so is the internet — which fascinates Zhang: "I think that the future will hold only two types of organisation: online platforms, and those that rely on them". That is the philosophy that nudged Haier in a direction it has followed since 2012 in its fifth, and most recent, incarnation. It has gradually implemented its RenDanHeYi model with the goal of eliminating bureaucracy, taking down organisational walls, improving response time, and encouraging entrepreneurial thinking. This has brought stark changes. In one major decision, 12,000 middle-management positions were made redundant, and 2,000 ZZJYT became 4,000 micro-enterprises.

As the name indicates, these are small, autonomous companies run by employees. Most are around 15-strong, some are smaller, others have as many as 200. The employees — or entrepreneurs, as they are referred to — are solely responsible for the provision of products and services. They must keep their company afloat and ensure optimal customer care. Customers may be internal (micro-enterprises that deliver HR services to others in the organisation) or external (those who buy the fridges or microwaves). The micro-enterprises connect with each other and suppliers. They ensure the creation of a market-place where all companies are affiliated with the same online plat-forms to collaborate and co-operate.

Zhang impresses upon us the importance of this most recent devel-opment. "We create an organisation that puts entrepreneurship at its heart. Everyone can be their own CEO." Employees now had agency: they could take almost all their decisions without consulting superi-ors or breaking protocol. From HR to choosing leaders, determining the division of profits, and strategy, the power was in their hands. Haier has even started experimenting with shared ownership, with employees becoming shareholders of the micro-enterprise in which they work. It's willing to go all the way in the creation of a network of teams and has taken the next step: a network of companies.

The story of Haier's many transformations is inspiring. This is the sort of thing we set out to discover, and share, through our Bucket List. This is a company story that reads like an adventure tale, a journey from past to present — and the possible future — of organisational science. But what makes it even more gratifying is the unique model it brings for the people who work there. We want to delve deeper into the world of micro-enterprises after our conversation with Zhang, to uncover the nuts and bolts. We intend to find out if the system truly brings motivation and entrepreneurship to life.

One of the many micro-enterprises that we study is a company named Thunderobot. We speak to many Haier workers, among them Lu Kailin who, in his previous role, was responsible for the firm's

It is painfully obvious: the system in which many people still work was created for a stable, slow and predictable world that no longer exists.

laptop division. "I discovered a rising need for gaming-specific computers," he tells us. Kailin and his colleagues came up with a plan to address that need by creating gaming computers. It wasn't straightforward, but after "we worked out the kinks", the team wanted to develop it. Haier had created an internal investment platform, giving employees access to finance, the company name, the brand, and all connections. The micro-enterprise was able to scale benefits within the supply chain and access the in-house expertise of other divisions: finance, marketing, human resources. This was an incubation platform for start-ups.

Lu Kailin and his colleagues reaped the rewards. In the summer of 2013, their idea grew into Thunderobot, Lu and his fellows became entrepreneurs. In December of that year, the first laptop hit the market. It was a great success. "We sold 500 in the first five days," says Lu, "and during the second delivery, 18,000 orders were placed in 21 minutes." Revenue grew equally swiftly, and in 2017 it passed the €100 million mark. In recent years, external investors came to the table, and Thunderobot was ready to list. The project shows how Haier has developed, removed, shifted or manipulated boundaries to create a co-operative era. We ask Lu what effect all this had on him. "Never in a million years did I think I could create a company like this," he smiles. "Since the start of Thunderobot, I have been able to develop myself in so many ways. My previous employer would never have allowed me to do this. I share the motivation of every person in our team. Everyone is enterprising, proactive and involved. "It hasn't always been easy, and the personal responsibility has grown. We must continue to make difficult choices with salaries, shares, hiring and firing. All that is tricky, but it brings a great sense of satisfaction."

During later visits we hear more stories like Lu's and see where the unique structure of Haier leads: to entrepreneurship, motivation, and innovation. It is certainly paying off for the company. The success of the new enterprises is around 50 percent. If that doesn't sound impressive, consider that a mere eight percent of start-ups survive, let alone succeed[17]. Haier's growth over the past few years has been explosive. Thinking back to our conversations with Ruimin, we can see how his vision became reality. The idiosyncratic leader with the sledgehammer destroyed those fridges with a certain kind of love. And with each hammer blow, he also demolished the old system. A bumbling, bureaucratic organisation was replaced by a free-flowing, adaptable structure. Zhang has a metaphor to explain the 4,000 micro-enterprises. "We try to organise ourselves like a rainforest," he says. "Eventually, every empire will collapse. A rainforest, on the other hand, will continue."

The way in which Haier has arranged itself is comparable to a lot of other pioneers. After our journey to China, we encounter many that have discovered the same structure and benefitted from it. Employees are divided into small, autonomous teams, sometimes independent companies. They focus on a specific market, region, product, or customer. They are granted autonomy, the right to be entrepreneurs and pioneers. Ironically, some fall back into the perceived safety of a more familiar way of working as soon as growth occurs. Going through radical transformation is not easy, nor completed in a day. But when it is carried out successfully, it has a huge impact on the engagement of employees and the future.

It is painfully obvious: the system in which many people still work was created for a stable, slow and predictable world that no longer exists. Today the system falters and fails and it is time to find a new way forward. Imagine if bureaucracy was kept to the absolute minimum with no wasted days of boring, frustrating meetings and no more doing things just because your boss says so. Imagine how much more time you would have to do useful work and keep the client happy. The most extreme scenario: How about running your own start-up together with your team? What would that do for your motivation and involvement? How would you be able to pull this off? For answers, we interrogated many companies that have changed their corporate structure to bring liberty. Instead of the hierarchical pyramid, these pioneers create an environment of flexibility, speed, and involvement. The structure we encounter most often at progressive organisations is the network of teams. We have come across them in all shapes and sizes, and in a host of cultures and industries. We visited the nurses and carers at Dutch Buurtzorg, the builders of Breman, the IT-ers of Nearsoft, the developers of Smarkets, the financial advisors of Finext, the technicians of TMC, and the consultants at Swedish Centigo. They are all networks built out of small, autonomous teams and Haier, once a slow, bureaucratic nightmare, is a wonderful example.

CRISIS AS CATALYST

Zhang Rhuimin is not the only person who has managed to transform a company, to take it from nothing to something remarkable. We heard a similar story during our visit to Swedish firm Svenska Handelsbanken where, in the 1970s, Jan Wallander was at the helm during a crisis. The transformation took five years. During this period, pretty much everything was turned around – or upside-down. But since then, this progressive bank has flourished, with a well-oiled network of teams ticking and linking like the intricate workings of a clock. The principles of radical decentralisation — even now, decades later — run strong in Handelsbanken.

We would have loved to find out more from Jan Wallander himself, but he passed away in 2016. We were nonetheless able to get a good idea of the unique methods Handelsbanken employs by travelling to Amsterdam, where we met Jens Wiklund, CEO of Handelsbanken Nederland. During our visits, Wiklund painted a clear picture of the man who kick-started this way of working.

Svenska Handelsbanken provides universal banking services, including traditional corporate transactions, investment banking, and trading. It also offers retail banking and life insurance services and is one of the major banks in Sweden, with some 460 branches. Since the mid-1990s, Handelsbanken has expanded throughout Scandinavia and the Nordic countries, the Netherlands, the United Kingdom, Estonia, Latvia and Lithuania. From 2016, there has been more growth. During our first visit to the bank's Dutch headquarters, we are received by Jens Wiklund, dapper in a perfectly cut suit, wearing trendy glasses. He comes across as a typical banker and, when we walk through the offices, we see what appears to be a traditional bank. Visually, the organisation gives little away. But we are here to peer beneath the veneer. Wiklund has worked here for 20 years, he tells us, before launching into the story of the transformational journey that Jan Wallander began.

"The adventure starts in 1970, when Wallander was appointed CEO," Wiklund tells us. "Handelsbanken was going through a crisis." Wallander's brief was challenging: he had to pull the company back from the brink. The starting point was becoming familiar to us. The organisation was centralised, the ever-growing head office taking all decisions. Those at the top decided the direction, and the employees had to deliver. One thing was clear, even from the outset: the traditional way of working does not provide employees with many rewards or much to aspire to. People believed (and some still do) that a strong, centralised, hierarchical structure would lead to good decisions and smooth running. The assumption was that the more people involved in the decision-making process (mainly those higher on the ladder), the better that decision would be. In practice, the opposite is true — as Handelsbanken was finding out.

It took the bank's leaders up to two months to take decisions on issues such as whether a customer should be granted a loan. This could have been a snapshot of our former working life, and we could relate. He recounted the tale of opulent headquarters, where those in power had dominion over everything — often via countless central-ised departments. Bureaucratic ditherings and administrative nonsense were seen as evidence of an organisation at work. Everything was arranged through head office: marketing, HR, finance, legal, planning, strategy, audit. There were a hundred groups and departments dealing with development and "improvement" projects. These were mainly concerned with generating a never-end-ing stream of memos with instructions on how each part of the bank should carry out its daily work. Know-it-all policies were issued by people who had never worked in any of the departments. This cost money and did little to generate anything other than more layers of bureaucracy. What money was made came through the efforts of employees in direct contact with customers.

But the centralised decision-making meant that, although the local branches knew their customers, they did not have the authority to take any meaningful decisions. "This not only frustrated the front line, it disturbed the newly appointed Jan Wallander," Wiklund tells us. "That is why Handelsbanken went in search of a new model. A model that displayed trust in the qualities and talents of employees."

The bank took a new path. The transformation that Wallander initi-ated was aimed at decentralisation. The power had to be diverted to local departments – and fast. That was where the money was being made." The head office culture was dismantled. The process was hindered and complicated by those in power, who were reluctant to release their death grip on the tiller. "From the moment he was appointed," says Wiklund, "Jan was aware that he had to set a good example. As the highest-ranking individual, he had to show that he was not just a man of pretty words. He had to show he meant it."[18]

Wallander did this by refusing to unilaterally take any major decisions after he had announced the decentralisation. If clients approached him directly, he would refer them to the local branches. "You can come to me," he would say, "but only the local branch can make a decision on this. I can put you in touch, but that might be the long way around."[18] The new CEO limited himself to small, personal changes to the day-to-day running of the bank — a modest stance which was, paradoxically but perhaps predictably, the start of bigger transformations. More radical actions were to shake-up the status quo, but always with the input and consent of the local branches. The sluggish giant was divided into smaller, more agile components. The local branches had small teams of 10 employees, but together they formed one large network. At the time of writing, Handelsbanken has 800 offices and 12,000 employees; each branch has genuine autonomy.

But deconstruction wasn't enough. To hammer home Wallander's commitment, it was forbidden for head office departments to communicate with local branches via memo. Groups were disbanded, as were centralised budgeting processes. Local branches no longer had to abide by the budgets of other departments. The creation of long-term visions, strategic plans and marketing campaigns now fell within their authority. Anything unnecessary went into the bin, and departments that couldn't accept the changes were disbanded. The new model stated that only the branches had the right to decide which products would be offered to their customers. How they would present them, and at what price, was again their decision. The responsibility for staff policies also lay with the local branches. They had — and still have — complete authority on hiring and firing, salary levels, and promotion. The role of head office had changed to one of support rather than control.

Jens Wiklund tells us about his personal experience. "To ensure that the local banks function to the best of their abilities, we get access to all relevant information. There is a slightly competitive element to this, where all branches are compared in terms of cost-to-income ratio. There are also other indicators, such as trends in volumes, customer numbers and audit ratings that branches and regions look at to gauge the development of a healthy business. The goal is constant striving for a better score." This competition is transparent: everyone has access to performance figures. Each month the local branches receive an overview on how they are performing, stirring healthy competition. This has proven beneficial for them and for Handelsbanken as a whole.

There is a collective responsibility. We saw this in the micro-enterprises of Haier, and other companies that use one or more of such criteria to measure the performance of autonomous teams. These parameters — such as customer satisfaction, billable hours, delivery times, growth, revenue and profit — must be objective and equal, so performance can be measured and compared one-on-one. More often-than-not, we have found that teams acquire their own secrets of success. They carry the responsibility for profits, income and expenses which are clear indicators of progress – as are purpose, customer satisfaction and productivity. The lists, published internally, ensure a feeling of pride for teams that are performing well and inspiration for those that aren't. Employees and team members learn for themselves how best to improve their performance without pressure.

The transformation process has provided Handelsbanken with good things. Decades of success in the Scandinavian market have given it the strength and resilience to become one of the fastest-growing banks in the Netherlands and in the United Kingdom. On a recent visit to Handelsbanken, we spoke with the then CEO, Anders Bouvin. He told us what the radical decentralisation has meant from his perspective. "Unlike a lot of other banks, we survived the financial crisis of 2008 fairly well," he said. "We had a minimum of 12 percent return on investment. Our yearly growth has been, on average, 15 percent — which is not something that many banks have been able to match."

Perhaps more importantly, Handelsbanken has a high rate of customer satisfaction[19] — and no bank in the world has a higher credit rating[20]. Bloomberg calls it the strongest bank in Europe; high praise indeed. The network-of-teams structure is just as beneficial in the world of European banking as it is on the vast factory floors of China.

The network-of-teams structure is just as beneficial in the world of European banking as it is on the vast factory floors of China.

PIONEERING PRACTICES FROM AROUND THE GLOBE

The lessons learned during our visits to Haier and Handelsbanken are reinforced by many other pioneers. They understand that employees need autonomy and trust in order to perform well. Often after reaching a total of 30 to 50 employees (sometimes before), organisations feel the need to centralise. Managers are appointed, functional departments created, formal rules and procedures set up, and weekly alignment meetings planned. Everything will be done to cling to the illusion of control. Unfortunately, people start to moan about the growing bureaucracy and control mechanisms.

Progressives tackle this differently. Before they reach critical mass – 10 to 15 employees – they divide into two autonomous teams within the same network. As soon as one reaches the critical point, it divides again. Growth is organic. The idea is simple, but implementation won't always be easy. The secret is to motivate the teams to keep everything running well and ensure the proper and healthy functioning of the network. Consider the seven other trends described in this book. An inspiring mission allows teams to work as one with everyone playing their part (an important source of motivation). The teams are often multidisciplinary to reflect the tasks expected. They are responsible for the functionality of their mini-company, represent the point of contact for customers and must ensure that all issues are resolved. This often brings not only benefits to the client but also increases the engagement and motivation of employees. Although all this may sound utopian, it does result in pressure. When shit hits the fan, the team must resolve problems by themselves.

With this intricate, growing network the question arises: How can their work be coordinated efficiently and yet avoid the trap of countless meetings? The answer is to ensure that as much information as possible is available. This calls for an IT system that has been developed to allow effective communication. Buurtzorg, a health care organisation we will touch upon later, has a special and very active intranet that all teams must join. They share news here but may also ask other teams for help. Buurtzorg organises a yearly congress where people get the chance to take part in workshops. Spotify has guilds, groups of employees who work in different teams but share expertise and interests. They meet on a regular basis, and while most guilds are work-related, some focus on hobbies and leisure.

There is a middle way, while others seek out the radical extremes. Here is an overview of possible structures. The first is the least radical, the fifth the most. But they are all improvements.

LEVEL 1 INVERTED PYRAMID

The days of frustrating and unrealistic vertical command-and-control communications are numbered. Create a renewed structure by upending this pyramid. Progressives take this step convinced that, in the main, it is the employees on the work floor that create added value. An inverted pyramid means that employees work pretty much as before but will understand that the organisation supports them. This pyramid still has managers making most of the decisions, but they do so believing that they are assisting employees closest to the client, product, or service. The leaders and head office are there to help the employees.

LEVEL 2 AUTONOMOUS TEAMS IN PYRAMID

Many progressives regard the inverted pyramid as obstructive and inflexible. To counter this they may create small, autonomous teams in certain areas. The trend may start in the IT department with the "Agile" way of working. At Swedish Spotify, IT developers – who make up a third of the company – form rootlike teams: small, intertwined, but autonomous. These have considerable responsibility for the end result and determine how they work: some choose to manage themselves – others work with a permanent leader. The rest of the employees work mainly in support functions based on a traditional hierarchy.

LEVEL 3 FLAT ORGANISATION WITH AUTONOMOUS TEAMS

The logical next step is to split the pyramid into autonomous teams, but for some that's too much, too soon. An interim solution is to create a flat organisation with minimal management layers. Handelsbanken has just three. The most important is comprised of the branches in direct contact with clients. The other layers are the regional offices and head office in Stockholm. The autonomous teams determine how they work, where they work, and with whom they work.

LEVEL 4 NETWORK OF TEAMS

Those that do dare destroy the pyramid, organise themselves in a network that is waited on by a small but efficient "head office". Buurtzorg has over 1,000 autonomous teams served by only 50 people. There is only one layer of hierarchy above the teams. Other examples include IT company Nearsoft, from Mexico; a group of production companies in the north of Spain; and the Municipality of Hollands Kroon. This structure allows the teams to determine their own way of working and carry full responsibility. In most cases, they ensure that multidisciplinary teams don't exceed 10 to 15 employees.

Divide the teams based on region, product, service, (or client), and ensure an efficient IT system allows employees to work together well. Make sure you have a group of coaches (without decision making privileges) that can assist if called upon. Would you like more entrepreneurship? Create a healthy form of competition and give the teams skin in the game. They become little companies that decide when and where they work, how, and with whom.

:VEL 5 ECOSYSTEM OF MINI-COMPANIES

The true radicals go one step further: as well as creating the network of mini-organisations by providing part ownership, an online platform is built to give access to stakeholders. This is exactly what Haier does with 70,000 employees organising themselves in over 4,000 mini-companies spread across multiple online platforms. They worry about internal competition as well as pressure from external stakeholders. For example: Is the HR team fulfilling expectations? If not, an external party is brought in. This dynamic ensures that only the teams that add real value will remain. The role of top management is still to determine the long-term strategy, but other than that they focus mainly on investing in the mini-companies they believe in and funding the start-ups.

How many layers of management does your business have, and how many of those should go? Is there a pyramid that could be reshaped into something more productive? What do you need to get things moving? How can you create opportunities? Take a good look at your organisation, because – as you're about to see – you don't have to be CEO to begin.

CHAPTER 3

FROM DIRECTIVE TO SUPPORTIVE LEADERSHIP

It's impossible to ignore the reputation of Ari Weinzweig, CEO of Zingerman's Community of Businesses since 1982. The community comprises nine companies that focus on the food industry. Each has an area of speciality, and those in charge part-own the businesses. Paul Saginaw and Weinzweig opened a sandwich bar in 1982 and this is where it all began. Nowadays, the group consists of a bakery, cheese factory, roadside restaurant, confectionary factory, Korean restaurant, mail-order company, training office, and coffee-roasting house. The group employs 700 people and generates a revenue of $70 million per year.

Rumour has it that every night Weinzweig does the rounds at one of his restaurants, pouring water for guests. This gesture sounds humble but impressive; is it true, and if so, does it have any real value? Equipped with a healthy dose of scepticism, we add Zingerman's to our Bucket List. During an elaborate road trip through the north-east of the United States (where, among others, we meet "Why guru" Simon Sinek, Menlo Innovations CEO Richard Sheridan, and Ross School of Business academics Chris White and Esther Kyte) we put Ari Weinzweig's reputation to the test. Will he be there, pouring water every night? We make an unannounced visit to the restaurant the evening before our scheduled meeting.

We arrive at Zingerman's around dusk, ready for dinner as well as observation. The name of the establishment is displayed in neon letters in handwritten style. An arrow points to a small subtext below the main title: "Really Good American Food". Lovely. We're hungry. Two conifers, reaching almost to the roof, flank the entrance. It is a one-storey building with a high ceiling and round lights hanging a metre or so above the heads of diners. We like the informal mood and cosy setting. We are shown to a table and sit back to get a view of the man and the water-pouring myth.

It doesn't take long to spot Weinzweig: dark, greying curls, a few days' stubble and silver earrings. And behold: he carries a jug of water, and he's going from table to table. We introduce ourselves and chat briefly, but he is a man on a mission: "I must move on guys, people are getting thirsty. See you tomorrow!" We are served shortly after, and yes, the food is good.

TRENCH WARFARE

Why are we so eager to obtain confirmation that effective leadership can be different? Why do we search for leaders that dare to be so? Because we have experienced the consequences of bad leadership where it was the rule – rather than the exception – that meetings were dominated by managers who, often visibly uneasy, clearly thought they must have the last word. Opinions were only valued when they originated from the lips of those with the biggest salaries. Those in the trenches were constantly overruled by leaders who had no clue what was going on. Consider the yearly appraisal meetings where a manager evaluates your performance without ever touching base to see how you're doing. Or targets established by a management oblivious to workplace realities. And how about the supervisor with a fancy company car and massive corner office, while the rest work themselves into an early grave? It drove us bonkers, and we're not the only ones. Research tells us that 50 percent of employees quit because of concerns about their manager[21].

The day after our restaurant visit, in the weak morning sun, we find Ari Weinzweig outside Zingerman's Coffee Company and join him for a double espresso. He tells us how it all started. The Zingerman Community of Businesses is heavily influenced by Weinzweig's interest in anarchy. He sees many parallels with his views on leadership. "What appeals to me when it comes to the anarchistic way of thinking," he says, "is the free mind, the free choice, the taking of initiatives, the working together, the creativity and the caring for the whole group. I assume we are all equal, and that everyone needs to be treated as such. Everybody is creative and intelligent by nature, and capable of great things. We must lead by supporting others, not by commanding. I'm not about bringing down current leaders. I'm about every employee being able to take on a suitable role of authority. Only then will everyone be able to effectively carry out their duties."

This sounds wonderful, but we want to know how Weinzweig makes this happen. After coffee, we follow him back to Zingerman's Roadhouse and he tells us about the monthly onboarding sessions. He tries hard to attend each one, but anytime that's not possible, fellow founder Saginaw steps up. When we enter the restaurant, six new employees are seated around a table. We are invited to stay for the session. We see a man in his element: filled with passion, he explains the history, mission, and core values. With frequent doses of humour, we hear inspiring stories and practical tips about life at Zingerman's as he focuses on food, service and finance. Weinzweig rips apart a large, freshly baked loaf and hands pieces to the employees. He talks about the origin of the bread, why they serve this type, and how it is made. People feel, smell, and eventually taste it, eyes closed. It's like an introductory course on mindfulness. Afterwards, Weinzweig makes it clear how much his organisation respects food. Then it is time for questions. For two hours, the employees quiz him.

After the welcome session it is time for our own questions. Ari explains his motivation. "Personnel onboarding is one of the most important things we do. It does not matter how much we grow, we are honoured whenever someone comes to join our business. The attentive and personal welcoming of our latest employees is the least we can do." These practices work only if leaders truly believe in this approach and then act on it. This man has an international reputation in the field.

"Paul and I need our staff way more than they need us. We have always known this. Without them here to provide great service, we'd probably still be at our little sandwich shop. Wonderful things happened over these past 30 years simply because a great number of intelligent, hard-working people gave us the chance to lead them. No leader will ever be truly productive without the people to make their vision a reality. Leaders without committed followers are doomed to fail."

What appeals to me when it comes to the anarchistic way of thinking is the free mind, the free choice, the taking of initiatives, the working together, the creativity and the caring for the whole group.

— Ari Weinzweig

Statistics and studies bear this out: a reported 65 percent of employees hate their boss so much that they would rather change their position and work with another manager than receive a pay rise. Bluntly put, the cost of bad management (in the United States alone) is estimated at $310 billion per annum. Zingerman's is built on this philosophy. The founders have not had to go through a transformation phase to rid themselves of traditional patterns. But during our travels we also see companies that radically change course, moving from directive to supportive leadership.

TEA AND TELLY IN LONDON

We had heard about British broadcasting network UKTV, and its rebellious CEO Darren Childs. UKTV is a partnership between the BBC and Discovery Channel and is one of the biggest broadcasting companies in the country, employing some 300 people. Founded in 1992, UKTV spent its first 20 years re-running BBC programmes, but now produces many of its own. Childs moved across from the BBC in 2010 to lead the company. UKTV had been through a radical transformation, our curiosity was awakened, and we arranged to visit. Under a blanket of grey clouds and the ever-present English rain we take an early morning walk through London, eventually arriving at an impressive building at its heart.

The fancy marbled reception area with its high ceiling feels like the most corporate place we have visited in a long while. Our sceptical nature is alerted and to find out more, we walk to the large counter, announce our presence, and wait. An employee welcomes us, and we are whisked upstairs. When we enter the offices, we are pleasantly surprised. The old-fashioned corporate atmosphere has given way and we seem to have stumbled into a parallel universe. The design is wonderful, with informal workplaces and circular sofas. In the open kitchen, we see people preparing their breakfast. The ceiling beams and pipes are exposed, and staff are working from comfortable, egg-shaped chairs. It all feels pleasantly informal and we are given an extensive tour. The words *"Create, Learn, Influence, Challenge and Collaborate"* adorn the walls: the core values. There is a large central staircase creating an open space between floors. The studios are also located in this building. The distance between those that manage the programming and the place where the programmes are made is purposely minimised. This flows from one of UKTV's slogans: "Tearing down hierarchy by design."

After the tour we meet Childs, dressed in a suit (without a tie). We enjoy a cup of tea – it is England after all – and ask him how he was able to chart UKTV's voyage in such a positive manner. A lot has changed since he took over. "From the first moment, I noticed that the organisation was hopelessly antiquated. I knew it was doomed if we kept clinging to the traditional ways." Once appointed, he took control and quickly revitalised the old, stiff hierarchy to encourage employees to unleash their creativity. An important part of the change was the creation of a supportive culture. Directional and detached leadership had to disappear so team leaders could be at the service of employees.

The first step was symbolic. "Everything in the UKTV office is there to rid us of the command-and-control structures," he says. "We want to dismantle hierarchy by design, and part of this was achieved by fully redecorating the office. We took all managers out of their rooms." The underlying thought is familiar, but very much in contrast with the traditionalists who cling to the "personal office incentive". Those stylish directors' offices on the top floor seemed to conflict with common sense and insight. Why would you lock yourself in your office because of seniority? Does it not make more sense to be among your team members, to know what's going on and be better able to help them? "Yes," says a study by Harvard Professor Francesca Gino[25].

Gino shows that managers who isolate themselves gain less respect. That reasoning inspired UKTV to put a stop to the practice. "Offices barricade the employees and that is exactly what we want to avoid," says Childs. "Instead we have open workspaces. Alongside that, we have areas that can be used for peace and quiet, and meetings."

The results are unequivocal with the employees we meet during our visit. "There is a more open atmosphere because leaders are closer to their teams. There is more and better communication between colleagues," says one. But just giving your office a makeover isn't going to be enough to break through. UKTV agrees and doesn't stop there. A first step has been made and there is time for the next move towards supportive leadership.

Childs tells us about the introduction of weekly "town-hall meetings". These are a recognised way to share knowledge and information. When we visited Googleplex, in California's Silicon Valley, we learned about the Thank God It's Friday meeting, when all 90,000 employees are invited to come together or phone-in. At Spotify, in Stockholm, we saw a similar ritual where founder and CEO Daniel Ek and colleagues go onstage to share company developments. But a rookie error was making attendance compulsory. Taking that route means you'll never find out if people find the meetings useful. The gatherings are not simply for standard management updates. At UKTV, an important part of the process is the sharing of adversity and mistakes. In this way, everyone can learn. "We want to give our employees the chance to receive all relevant information," Childs explains. "Employees can ask us questions: nothing is taboo." But he noticed that there had not been too many tricky ones. Most employees were not comfortable in bringing up the touchier subjects.

"That was one of the most difficult things," says Childs, "convincing people that it really is OK to ask anything because we want to be completely transparent." He came up with a simple but effective solution: a post-box decorated with a prominent white question mark. Anyone with a question, or wanting to share matters of a sensitive nature, was asked to write it down and put it in the box. It would be opened only during the meetings. All questions were answered there and then, with no prepared, politically correct answers or corporate propaganda. This became a powerful tool. "I open the box and read aloud whatever it says on the note. Then the leadership team and I try to answer honestly. This was one of the most important steps in creating a culture of supportive leadership. It sends a clear signal that we want transparency and brings their concerns to our attention. We demonstrate that we are there for them."

During the transformation, UKTV made another radical move. This time, it tackled evaluations and reviews. There were questions such as: how can you encourage managers to give total support to their teams? How do we recognise and reward appropriate behaviour? "Who should evaluate management performance?" Childs asks a question of his own. "Right: your team." The traditional top-down investigations were overhauled to provide that opportunity. This was not meant as a great embarrass-the-boss-session, rather a source of honest feedback. Every member of the team gives the manager a score for certain tasks. And UKTV goes a step further: the results are shared with everyone in the company. Sounds wonderful, but does this work? Childs understands our uncertainty. "It is not always easy for those managers who are underperforming," he admits, "but they get the necessary impetus to improve.

"Nobody wants to be the worst. Although it can be painful, the alternative is a team that must deal with bad leadership, and its consequences." That change is apparently working, given the recent performance of UKTV. Regular reviews have shown that employees are happier, more involved, and more creative. The company reaped rewards too: sick leave was drastically reduced, and in less than five years the company's market value had doubled.

Those in the trenches were constantly overruled by leaders who had no clue what was going on.

PIONEERING PRACTICES FROM AROUND THE GLOBE

Weinzweig and Childs are progressive leaders running companies in their own authentic way. They share many common values. Each person is unique, so there are many ways in which supportive leadership can be brought to life. But how do you succeed in creating this? What are the points to keep in mind? How can you adjust the way things work within your team? What insights did our other visits give us? Here are some rebellious ways in which progressives distinguish themselves. We start on simple ploys and work up to the more radical solutions.

LEVEL 1 BEWARE OF HIPPOS

This archaic style of leadership isn't just costing an enormous amount of money, it also leads to dubious work practices. We regularly experienced the HiPPO-effect (Highest-Paid Person's Opinion). This refers to the habit of siding with the highest-ranking officer (and therefore often the one drawing the top salary) and not acknowledging the person who has the most expertise, experience, or the brightest ideas. The traditional workplace tends to overlook the content of a problem simply to please the most senior person. The ineffectiveness of this has been scientifically proven.

A study carried out at the Rotterdam School of Management[22] shows that projects supervised by junior managers have a high success rate. Their colleagues feel more comfortable expressing themselves, less intimidated. Senior managers are as prone as anyone to blunders and giving them more say backfires.

Progressives do their best to avoid this in a direct and lighthearted way, for example by placing "Beware of HiPPOs" signs on the wall. A staff member of the UK's National Health Service (NHS) – inspired by our Bucket List experiences – warned those attending meetings to "park your hierarchy at the door". They saw progress in just a few days. People had the confidence to come forward with suggestions and dared to engage in discussions with senior staff. Moral of the story? Make decisions based on content, not the bringer of the content.

LEVEL 2 DESTROY THE IVORY TOWER

A fair number of traditional organisations shower privilege and status symbols on the higher ranks: reserved parking spaces, corner offices. These are hangovers from the Industrial Revolution. Hopefully, we can look back in a couple of years and wonder why on earth we used to do it that way.

Maintaining the ivory tower is not just outdated, it is bad for business. The tower undermines the pretty but often empty words in annual reports which proudly proclaim that "employees are the backbone of the business". Get rid of the nonsense and create a more inclusive environment. The inspiring leaders we met have paved the way. An excellent example is to be found at a group of 50 companies we visited in Bilbao, Spain. During the group's transformation, as we will see in a later chapter, they abandoned all privileges from day one.

LEVEL 3 EVALUATE YOUR MANAGER

Organisations espouse a desire for supportive leadership, but often little transpires. This is not surprising if the way in which you make judgments and dole-out rewards is unchanged. Progressives swap the top-down reward system for a bottom-up model.

Maintaining
the ivory tower
is not just
outdated,
it is bad
for business.

How can the boss ascertain how well a manager leads? A proper feedback system will listen to the people best suited to make that evaluation: team members. Rebellious organisations dare to do this. Leaders with the right stuff make these sessions open.

LEVEL 4 SPLIT MANAGERS

Hierarchy itself is not the problem. Artificial hierarchy is. When authority isn't based on competence or quality of leadership, the result is the dreaded Peter Principle – a concept that has been understood for decades but is still with us. Laurence J Peter's book of 1969[23] describes it well: "In a hierarchy every employee tends to rise to his level of incompetence."

Imagine you are a sales rep. and an incredibly good one. This does not go unnoticed. Boss and colleagues are so impressed that you are hailed as a real talent. And a talent deserves promotion: from now on, you are a sales manager! Naturally, you are pleased, and probably get an increase in salary or a bigger car. You have new responsibilities that make you pleasurably busy and fill you with importance. You can't wait to share this on your LinkedIn page.

But this sort of promotion doesn't make sense. Why take someone who excels in sales and give them the role of managing people? Management requires a different skillset. Being good at one thing does not necessarily mean that you'll excel at another. A study published in Harvard Business Review[24] came to the same conclusion. Many organisations we have visited make short work of the Peter Principle by creating multiple promotion tracks. If you're a great IT programmer, you don't necessarily need a management position as recognition. You can become an expert in your field and a mentor. Reward structures must be meaningful.

An organisation that is ace at doing this is the Polish IT company U2i, in Krakow. When we visited their office, we learned of their extraordinary approach. As employee Pawel Kozlowski said, "the only way to move up was to push somebody down the stairs". This diseased system has been put to pasture. The new way allows every employee to grow within his or her area of expertise.

LEVEL 5 CHOOSE YOUR LEADER

Why are inspiring leaders so thin on the ground? Perhaps our traditional way of organising leadership is at fault. Imagine a workplace where leaders are elected after providing a good example. Or where people can share their opinions and provide feedback without fear of consequences, where opinions are judged purely on content. This could improve the atmosphere as well as motivation and productivity. It's clear that the traditional way of management and leadership often stands in the way of success. In our search, we have had conversations with gurus such as Tom Peters, Frédéric Laloux and Isaac Getz. We have also spoken with radical leaders such as Kees Pater, CEO of the Dutch cookie factory Veldt, Jean-François Zobrist, former CEO of the French FAVI, Mario Kaphan, founder of the Brazilian Vagas.com, and CEO Bob Hutten of the eponymous Dutch catering company.

Of the 100-plus Bucket List organisations we have visited, most have one thing in common: a lack of directive leadership. Instead we find supportive senior staff that lead by example, who ask their employees the best way to help and support them. They show an admirable combination of authenticity, modesty, rebelliousness and stubbornness. They have a clear vision and inspire their people to action. At the same time, they are available for feedback and criticism. They listen to the ideas of those on the front line. This is Supportive Leadership.

"If you want to be a leader, you'd better find some followers." That motto may be tongue-in-cheek, but it's a wonderful piece of advice. Letting employees choose their own leader is one of the most rebellious solutions. Those that have the strength to do this will be rewarded. Create a voting process, allow people to select their mentors, or go for continuously changing leadership; the way you achieve this doesn't matter, just go for it.

Swiss IT company Haufe Umantis was the most radical in this regard. All positions of power are democratically chosen - even that of the CEO. This might not be something to start tomorrow, but it is a powerful example of radical change for the better. The beauty of selecting leadership is that those who are chosen can really lead. And if things don't work out the team can always find a replacement...

CHAPTER 4

FROM PLAN & PREDICT TO EXPERIMENT & ADAPT

My name is Pablo Aretxabala, I am part of K2K Emocionando, a team of seven people that — for more than 10 years — has been dedicated to the transformation of businesses into New Style of Relationships (in Spanish, Nuevo Estilo de Relaciones, or NER). NER originated in 1991, when Koldo Saratxaga was appointed General Co-ordinator of the Irizar Co-operative: a high-end bus company that was established in 1889 in Ormaiztegi, a small town in the Basque Country, as a manufacturer of carriages and stagecoaches.

In 1991 Irizar was technically bankrupt and there was strong internal conflict. In a few years the company took a radical turn and thanks to its innovative management became an amazing success story. In 2006, Koldo created the K2K Emocionando team to develop and adapt NER for all organisations. Since then, there have been several dozen profound corporate transformations that we have led here. Probably the best known are those of the 26 companies that nowadays make up NER group and employ some 2,000 people.

NER is about making people effective and the true centre of organisations – working with absolute transparency, trust, freedom, and responsibility. Those that have implemented the new style of relationships have no hierarchical structure of any kind, no elements of control, no power struggles, no dark zones. Instead we have self-managed teams, responsibility, commitment, initiative and shared decision-making.

We advocate the choice of leaders by the teams, the elimination of existing controls. We recommend the dissemination of performance information to everyone, the removal of salary imbalances, decision-making by assemblies, recruitment and evaluation of new employees by their potential colleagues, the prohibition of dismissals for economic reasons, and making everybody aware of all financial facts concerning the company.

NER organisations have a strong social commitment, contributing 2.5 percent of profits and two percent of staff working time to community projects. Of the 150 initiatives developed, we are especially proud of: Lur Denok (in Basque this means "the land of all") and Hurbilekojalea Dendak ("the shops of the people who eat local and organic products"). These are two projects of production, distribution and commercialisation of organic food in which almost 300 partners are involved.

"I do not want to overwhelm you with information but hope that this message has aroused your curiosity. Hoping to establish contact; I send you an affectionate greeting on behalf of the K2K team."
Pablo Aretxabala

Our research had been going on for about 18 months when, on a random Monday morning, we checked our inbox to find this fascinating email from Pablo with the unpronounceable surname. We were immediately hooked.

The story he related, and the questions it raised, stirred our little universe in a slightly unsettling way. Dozens of traditional companies transformed into progressive organisations? Did they all operate without artificial hierarchy, where teams could choose their own leaders and the decision-making process was shared? And were they all within the relatively compact region of Bilbao, in northern Spain? How on Earth could we have missed this one, in all our hunting for progressive companies? How come we had not heard this story before? And just who was this man with the enigmatic (and equally unpronounceable) name of Koldo Saratxaga? We were slightly abashed that we were not already familiar with this pioneer, or with NER. Questions, questions, and further questions; we had to find out more, and a month later we were on a plane to Bilbao.

Our plan was to follow our by-now normal procedure, and spend some time with the K2K team, hear Pablo's stories at first-hand, and visit these radical companies...

IN BASQUE COUNTRY

We arrive at Bilbao airport to find Pablo waiting for us. He's a friendly chap aged about 50. After brief introductions, we travel to our first destination: a metalworking company. In its office — transformed a few years ago by the K2K Emocionando Consultancy — we meet Koldo Saratxaga. He is the founder of K2K, which has transformed 70 dysfunctional organisations into progressive and dynamic workplaces. The group has members across diverse industries including engineering, manufacturing, law, cybersecurity, and education. It has a presence in 60 countries and combined annual revenues in excess of €400 million.

Koldo is an impressive figure, wise and amiable, about 70 years old with longish white hair. His voice is sonorous and soothing... but he doesn't speak English. Fortunately, Pablo is on-hand to translate. Koldo immediately pushes the metaphorical rewind button and takes us back to the early 1990s when he joined the Irizar Group. With more than 3,000 employees, Irizar is the leading builder of coach bodies in Spain, with a market share of over 40 percent and a turnover of more than €550 million a year. The group's products are distributed around the world, and Irizar operates five production plants in Spain, Morocco, Brazil, Mexico and South Africa. "Irizar was in deep crisis," he says. "The leadership had changed twice within a year, and employee morale was at rock-bottom. Its survival was in the balance. Sales were negligible, losses intimidating; the company image was poor." Koldo knew it was time for a radical change.

It was vital that the workers themselves rebuild Irizar; Koldo did not intend to issue dictates or instruct anyone to chase targets. "I let go of the naïve belief that the world in which we work can be predicted," he says, "or that every detail can be planned. I embraced the idea of creating a workplace that was adaptive, resilient and responsive. I dispensed with the false comfort that making detailed plans can bring – and falling back on the notion of control – in what was a highly uncertain environment. Detailed annual plans may have been standard practice a hundred years ago, but in our modern world this is far from ideal." We no longer live in the era where, every day, an identical Model T would roll off Henry Ford's production line. We can no longer predict with any certainty what the next calendar year will bring. Change, as they say, is the only constant: today's world is a very different one to that of just a few decades ago.

The result? Organisations have become more complicated. Far from solving the problem of complexity, we worsened it with bureaucracy[26]. This is not the whole story, of course. Many companies fall into the trap that Koldo neatly sidestepped. They attempt to predict the future and try to wrest control from chaos. The most painful and frustrating signs of this folly usually come in the annual budgeting rounds. Anyone who has worked in a large or medium-sized company will be familiar with these. The misery of meetings to set budgets or decide what actions will (in theory) yield the best results.

This pattern of bureaucracy has become a ritual in many companies. Managers hunch behind laptops displaying Excel files, effectively casting bones or reading chicken entrails in a bid to know what the coming year will bring. During the resulting management shutdowns, office politics, point-scoring and petulant negotiations are the only predictable outcomes. When the shutdown is over, the business is led by the nose along the path of the negotiated budgets. This "managing-by-numbers" ensures little, other than that employees are prompted to take irrational decisions rather than use common sense. We found evidence of this in our previous incarnations on the corporate treadmill. The most glaring example of the system's flaws? That employees, come the end of the financial year, would start

Bureaucracy has become a ritual in many companies. Managers hunch behind laptops displaying Excel files, effectively casting bones or reading chicken entrails in a bid to know what the coming year will bring.

ordering all sorts of unnecessary items to use up the appointed budgets – for fear that if they didn't, next year's would be smaller.

This impulsiveness and anxiety is so deeply rooted that it has come to seem normal. Setting budgets and planning can sap an enormous amount of time and energy - and cost a lot in financial terms too. Ford Motor Company once estimated that planning and budgeting processes cost around $1.2 billion each year[27]. That's a lot of waste. This recognisable and recurring misery is based on the odd idea that it is possible to predict the future. Spoiler alert: it isn't. It is time to accept, and embrace, change as something that is unpredictable, often surprising, and random. The old "we've been doing it this way for years" approach is no longer acceptable. We went in search of companies that understand this — and found plenty.

To be clear, we're not talking about the trending "agile methodo-logies" that companies currently strive for or claim to have as a goal. While the foundations of the "agile" movement are sound, and valuable, the way many companies practice it is simply wrong. Many labour under the impression that if you do daily stand-ups, use a truckload of Post-its and appoint a scrum master, you've created an entirely new way of looking at the workplace. Unfortunately, that isn't the case. The pioneers we've visited have moved beyond buzzwords and hype to employ healthy experimentation: new products, revised services, alternative ways to carry out work. Even in highly regulated sectors, they have managed to embrace flexibility and cope with an ever-changing environment.

Koldo Saratxaga introduced methods that were in stark contrast to traditional wisdom. "I focused on creating a flexible, adaptive, and engaging workplace," he says. "We needed to create an environment where it was acceptable to experiment, and quickly adapt should the situation call for it.

"I first got rid of the hierarchical pyramid, with all its prediction and command-and-control mechanisms. I created an almost flat organisation that consisted of multidisciplinary, self-managed teams. They resembled mini-companies within the bigger entity. There were more than 120 of these, most consisting of four or five people and a team leader. Team members were assigned to projects and were able to elect their leaders. Teams performed a specific task within a certain time-frame and were encouraged to start every project with an open mind. Most workers were part of more than one team, which provided them with fresh challenges, and diverse goals." Koldo did not stop there; he transformed the physical working space as well. "We relocated the manufacturing and service facilities to one floor. This provided staff from the various departments with the opportunity to get to know one another. We dispensed with personal offices and created common rooms which any team, or team member, could use."

To ensure that the culture of experimentation took root, Koldo allowed workers a high level of autonomy. "The mini-companies could, for example, set their own objectives and time schedules. We also removed most of the old control mechanisms, such as the clock that monitored people as they entered and left the factory. Everyone was trusted to complete an eight-hour workday, but your attendance was only known by your closest colleagues. Our model at Irizar was partly chaotic, but generated order through self-organisation. Everyone had a good degree of freedom — and a corresponding amount of responsibility. Each worker was the owner of his or her own relationships and decisions." Evaluations were based solely on team performance; individual evaluations were avoided. Koldo used the power of transparency by instructing the mini-companies to make their objectives and results known throughout the organisation.

The success of his approach was staggering. By implementing a system focused on experimentation, adaptation and freedom, Koldo had created an empowered workforce. The new model provided Irizar with annual growth of around 24 percent — for 14 consecutive years. During Koldo's tenure, revenue grew from €24 million to €310 million. Growth was so strong that Irizar was able to open plants in other countries. Production went from 226 coaches a year to 1,600. Not only was capacity increased, but production time fell from an average of 38 days to just 14.

For Koldo, however, the success at Irizar wasn't enough. "That story had inspired people around the globe, and many of them wanted to visit our factories. More than 4,000 people came each year." But these visits didn't create the hoped-for "viral effect". "Many people came up with arguments to show why our approach could never work given their circumstances. I became so frustrated by the never-ending list of excuses that I set out to prove them wrong. I started K2K Emocionando to encourage others. And I had good reason."

He decided that K2K Emocionando would help transform traditional organisations into progressives. "Leaders should create an environment in which employees can excel," says Koldo. "An experimental and entrepreneurial environment is stimulated. Our approach was radical and based on a list of logical principles. We first had to get rid of the old command-and-control mindset. One of the most important principles of our approach is to see everyone in the workplace as equal, from the guy that sweeps the floor to the owner. So, from day one, all privileges are eliminated — as you can see in this metalworking company," he adds, gesturing to the surrounding workspace.

"Just look around you. There are no private offices, no executive dining rooms, no reserved parking, nor any bonuses or incentives for individual performance, and no special access to information."

After removing privileges, the consultants redesign every organisation into a network of teams. "We started to reorganise into a system based on products, services, regions, clients, and processes," Koldo says. "Once the network is in place, each team elects its own representative. These leaders, however, have no power, and don't get extra salary.

"Teams can opt to spread this role across two or more people and replace the leader at any time. The leaders merely co-ordinate and communicate with other teams." At K2K, not only is everyone equal, but each has an equal responsibility. "We put a stop to top-down decision-making and ensure that the process is based on shared responsibility," says Koldo. "Every decision taken involves the people it affects." In a true experimental and entrepreneurial atmosphere, decision-making must be shared, Koldo believes. "And for this, it's crucial to have full transparency, including financial information, for all involved. We make salary levels transparent, as well as team commitments and results."

Why do they do this? To continuously involve employees in running their own company, and to ensure a sense of fairness. "Just as you can see here. This helps to align goals." But it's important to remember that none of those targets are dictated top-down, nor are they controlled. They are all fully self-set by the members to ensure team play. Commitment meetings are held every two to three weeks, where results are reviewed. These measuring and tracking mechanisms are designed to give teams access to real-time information about their performance.

"I wouldn't
old way, but
understand
Having a boss
you what to do
advantages.
know, the harder
in some ways;
ignorance is

go back to the

you have to

it's not easy.

who tells

has its

The more you

things become

sometimes

bliss."

K2K also suggests companies hold monthly and quarterly meetings to give a wider understanding of the financial details and of how the business is run.

Pablo takes up the explanation. "While much of the world is about finance, not many people truly understand it," he says. "Even in business, most people can't properly read a balance sheet or profit-and-loss account. How can they set goals and targets, if they don't understand the basics of running a company? This is why we first teach everyone the basics in finance." Other control practices also vanished. "We move by goals and commitments, not by hours. And it is also perfectly fine to make mistakes, even if it leads to some chaos and frustration early on. Who hasn't made mistakes when starting something new?" Trial and error are part of learning, not something to be punished or discouraged.

When we walk around the workplace later that day, a few employees tell us how the changes have influenced them. "When we started here it felt a bit like leaving your parents' house to live on your own," said Leire Villoria Diez. "When you find an empty fridge it's up to you to sort it out. There is nobody telling you what to do or controlling you. You must start experimenting and figure out with your team the best way to achieve the desired results. In the end, you always manage."

Leire's colleague, Aitor Sanz, adds: "I wouldn't go back to the old way, but you have to understand it's not easy. Having a boss who tells you what to do has its advantages. The more you know, the harder things become in some ways; sometimes ignorance is bliss." The first steps towards a more progressive way of working are demanding. But over the years, K2K has proved that transformation is always possible, with the proper mindset and dedication. Pablo shares some of the results. "In the past 12 years we have supported more than 70 companies.

Researchers from the University of Basque Country found that in each case the financial results improved within the first two years. Outcomes depend on the character and style of the firm, but productivity has always improved – by an average of 40 percent. The salaries of the companies are 30 percent higher than the Basque Country average, and 40 percent above the Spanish national average. Absenteeism and accident rates are far lower."

THE ART OF MAKING MISTAKES

The stimulation of experiments is not unique to these Basque Country companies, of course. It's something we encountered in our visit to the Swedish music streaming company Spotify, founded by ex-hacker Daniel Ek and a few others. In recent years, Spotify has turned the industry upside-down – and grown steadily. By the time we visited the head office in Stockholm, it had a workforce of 3,000. Nothing stands still for long at Spotify, and 100 new employees are joining every month. Despite this, the company is forever experimenting and staying ahead of the competition. Daniel Ek's tongue-in-cheek motto speaks volumes: "We aim to make mistakes faster than anyone else."

Mistakes come naturally enough, but to incorporate the learning from them, and maintain the unique corporate culture of Spotify's early days of exponential growth, proved a challenge. All successful startups must deal with this, and not all emerge victorious. Growth and chaos often go hand in hand, and some try to manage this by increasing control and bureaucracy. That's a shame, because the breakthroughs that brought success start to falter. Their example has shown that things can be done differently. Spotify ticks all the boxes of a modern start-up. Music piped into every room, graffiti on the walls, comfy sofas with rainbow-coloured cushions, and a jumble of hanging art. But we haven't travelled all this way to study interior design and listen to music. We are here to get a better picture of Spotify's way of working. The engineers have formed into squads, tribes and guilds. It all sounds way more complicated than it is, and – to no one's surprise, perhaps – strongly resembles the network-of-teams model.

HR director, Katarina Berg, wearing a bright red blazer and even brighter smile illuminates us. "As basic units, we have self-steering teams of six to 12 developers. These are referred to as squads and resemble mini-corporations. Each squad has its own workspace and plan of attack. "We don't tell people how to do their jobs. The squads working co-operatively on a feature – for example, the music player or backing infrastructure – form what we call a tribe. You could think of the tribes as incubators for the mini-companies; they ideally consist of about 40 developers, and don't usually surpass 150 employees.

"To stimulate connections between the groups, we brought in chapters and guilds. Chapters are small groups of specialists from the same tribe that share their expertise. They form close-knit communities and meet for work-related discussions. Guilds stem from a similar rationale, but these are company-wide, and do their business in a more relaxed manner. There are hobby related guilds, from hiking to brewing beer and photography.

"There is one other important group I haven't mentioned: the coaches. Every squad has access to coaches who can help develop and improve work methods. That description is just a snapshot, of course. Our current way of working is unique, but by no means perfect. We are aware that we do not have all the answers, and with such rapid growth we encounter new challenges every day. This is a process of continuous discovery."

We quickly realise how important experimentation is to the Spotify culture. Walls are decorated with multi-coloured Post-its, and whiteboards indicate progress. Berg says that this too is to stimulate experimentation. "We place more value on innovation than predictability. Prediction can never be innovative. We are all about providing added value, not carrying out prefabricated plans. All our experiments are noted on the whiteboards. Teams regularly gather there to gauge progress. What experiments have been carried out? What have we learned from them? What comes next? The squads can reflect on what was working, and what has proven to be less effective."

This stimulates the teams to constantly try out and test new ideas. The philosophy is one of common sense and evaluation. "It really isn't complicated," Berg says. "We try to measure what the experiment can provide, and verify if it worked, or adds value. If that's a positive answer, we'll keep it. If not, we'll ditch it." This ensures that important decisions made by the squads are based on realistic data, not opinions or ego. The developers of Spotify enjoy a healthy measure of trust and responsibility. Making mistakes is acceptable as long as something is learned along the way. Some squads have a special Fail Wall to encourage learning from errors. Alongside these Fail Walls, internal blogs share successes and failures to create a culture of improvement, always driven by the employees themselves. "We would rather spend our time and energy on adjusting, and quickly recovering, than on futile attempts to predict the future."

PIONEERING PRACTICES FROM AROUND THE GLOBE

American academic Leon Megginson observed in his 1963 inter-
pretation of Charles Darwin's central thesis that it is neither the
strongest nor the smartest of the species that survives, but the most
adaptable. This is an essential insight for businesses struggling to
meet unprecedented challenges. Competition is changing, the
customer base is changing, the technology is changing; so is the
market. Systems no longer last for generations and may only be
useful for a few years, or even months. Businesses that become too
attached to the status-quo are often the ones who most fiercely
defend it. They should realise that they are the ones that will ultimately lose. Businesses that constantly experiment will be the
winners.

Progressives see this new reality not as a problem but as an exciting
challenge. They know that they will never "get there". In this process
of experimentation, speed is essential: rapid change requires rapid
response. "Progressives know that success belongs to the fast
learner. Spotify embraces this notion." Although at first glance the
group of companies from Bilbao and Spotify might not appear to
have much in common, you may be surprised. Both have been able to
adjust to this new reality of rapid change. This is exactly why progressive organisations abolish the old prediction and control
mechanisms. They say goodbye to the rigid budget cycle, stifling
coordination meetings, and the questionable decisions mindset.
They know that adaptability is a must and focus on building the
appropriate culture. The key to success is to experiment often, fail
quickly, and keep improving. Just to be clear: these pioneers know
that the most valuable experiments are the result of intense interac-
tion between employees, customers and other stakeholders. They

We place more
value on
innovation than
predictability.
Prediction can
never be
innovative.

— Katarina Berg

are not the result of a mystical view of the future by a group of over-paid consultants or astrologers.

Progressives pioneer alternative ways and are an important source of inspiration for ruthless experimentation and adaptation. They show the path to follow. Here is a starting point: once again, we look first at the easy steps.

LEVEL 1 RUTHLESSLY EXPERIMENT

Nike had it right all along. When it comes to experimentation the best advice is: just do it. Action is the most powerful antidote to the corporate disease of "analysis paralysis". To break through action is needed. Take inspiration from the factory workers from Bilbao and the developers at Spotify. Follow their lead and start experimenting yourself. Realise that change should no longer be a once-a-year event. It is a part of everyday work. It is always better to experiment and fail than never to try something new. An idea for a new product or service? Experiment! Improve your way of working? Experiment! Skip those useless alignment meetings? Experiment! Try out new ideas and make evidence-based decisions about how best to move forward.

Don't give up too quickly. Matt Perez, founder of Mexican IT company Nearsoft, inspired us with this principle: "We wish to create a culture of experimentation. So, when a person or team wants to experiment with something new – and there is enough internal support – they're free to give it a try. If we decide to go for it, we usually commit for at least one year. We want to learn and innovate by trial and error. See if it actually works."

LEVEL 2 KILL THE BUDGET CYCLE

Dispense with your annual management processes that are based on wild guesswork, involve fixed targets and largely revolve around office politics. Get rid of your detailed annual budgeting cycles, your fixed yearly targets and goals. If the Swedish bank Handelsbanken (with thousands of employees) can do this why shouldn't you? Only plan and forecast if it seems vital. In such cases, arrange the processes in a more dynamic way by establishing short-term (i.e. monthly or weekly) goals and rolling forecasts. Make sure everyone is aware of how the business attempts to make sense of those goals and allocate resources on demand where they seem to be most needed.

LEVEL 3 CREATE A "SAFE-TO-TRY" ENVIRONMENT

Experiment properly and fail masterfully. Whether you like it or not, the two belong together. You must ensure that people feel safe with this. Otherwise you'll end up nowhere. If they fail, they should be rewarded not punished. You're not going to punish your child for falling over when learning to walk, right? Look at experimentation in the same way. Without falling you'll never truly rise. Simply ask the question: "Is it safe enough to try?" That's all you need to know. Evaluate, learn, adapt. See it as progress. Various pioneers hold regular "Fuck-Up" events. People share their biggest disasters and tell the crowd what they have learned. Do you fancy holding such an event? Make sure the leaders are the first to share. Hand out awards for the best failures and create special moments to celebrate experimentation. This will create the environment you're looking for and encourage others. Experimentation should be fun and exciting, not threatening.

LEVEL 4 CROWDSOURCE EXPERIMENTS

Set up a crowdsourcing platform and invite employees to join. Create a bottom-up movement. Large-scale change programmes fail 70 percent of the time. The problem is that they are often initiated and managed from on-high but seldom supported by frontline staff – who will effect the change. Build a crowdsourcing platform that allows anyone to do something new – like the factory workers at Haier. Invite everyone to participate and come up with suggestions, let them recruit their fellow rebels and launch the most popular experiments.

LEVEL 5 REBEL TIME

Go further, give everyone the time they need to rebel. There are many ways to go about this. One is to create dedicated experimentation time through the appointment of full-time rebels – a select bunch who constantly push things forward. At Spotify developers enjoy a "10 percent hack time" to work on anything they want. A Belgium governmental department encourages employees to devote 15 percent of their time in this way. Google used to have the famous 20 per cent rule where employees could spend a fifth of their time on self-initiated projects. With wonderful results: some of their most important products like Gmail and AdSense came from this.

CHAPTER 5

FROM RULES & CONTROL TO FREEDOM & TRUST

"You must visit the man with the funny stories and silly shoes." This is something we hear surprisingly often, and in various places, on our travels. Legend has it that this man works in an unusual organisation, and that he is the driving force behind the creation of one of the most remarkable government bodies. That sounds promising. We decide to track him down and find out what makes him tick.

Our target is Frank van Massenhove, of the Belgian Ministry of Social Security. His books and the stories we find on the internet are intriguing, and our curiosity grows on the drive to Brussels. Can it be true that there is a ministry where civil servants decide for themselves where, when, and even how many hours they work? Where there is not even a record of timekeeping? A ministry without recurring meetings? We have visited our fair share of remarkable workplaces, but this sounds unbelievable.

We arrive at the city centre and park close to the Finance Tower where the ministry is located; it looks cold and ruthlessly corporate: 36 storeys of glass and a total lack of atmosphere. We report to reception and a friendly lady guides us to one of the building's lower levels. Although we are heading for the basement, we emerge into a light, colourful and modern space. Van Massenhove soon arrives, and our first impression is that he looks like Lambik, a Flemish comic book character from the series Suske And Wiske. He has a wide smile, sparkling eyes, and the silly, shiny blue shoes and clashing socks we have heard so much about.

"I got the job as head of the organisation in 2002, mainly because I lied during my interviews," is his candid opening line. This is not something you'd expect from the chairman, but while the lie was substantial, it was white. "If I was completely honest about my plan not to take all the decisions myself and give employees the power, I wouldn't have been appointed. So, I told them what they wanted to hear. I said I was going to lead via command-and-control, show staff who's the boss, tell them how to do their jobs, and take all the important decisions myself. It worked a treat.

"One of the most common mistakes is to bring in the wrong managers, the kind who take full control. This feels 'safe', but it's lacking in trust – and employees are deprived of responsibility and ownership."

From Day One, Frank van Massenhove showed his inner rebel. "When I got the job, I did exactly the opposite of what I said," he smiles. "Nicely recalcitrant, I know. My goal was to build on foundations of freedom, trust, and responsibility. Why? I have different ideas about leadership than your average chairman. I wanted to introduce a new atmosphere, because I have more faith in the employees than I have in myself."

The difference here, we note, is not just the socks.

"Putting this into practice is not always easy," he continues, "especially considering the state of the ministry at that time. I arrived with a head full of ideas, but found a neglected, dusty organisation spread out over Brussels in four buildings. It was too sad for words. One of the departments was in an old car park, so you could have driven down the corridors. There were meeting rooms without windows. The four buildings each had their own corporate culture, depending on which floor you were on. Any similarities we found were negatives: endless rows of filing cabinets and a hierarchy better suited to the Sun King, Louis XIV.

"The internal communication system made me cringe, the IT systems rarely worked properly, and the people were unhappy and poorly motivated. They didn't dare to show any initiative, because they'd be shot down. Most struggled to explain exactly what their role was, and the service to the public was shocking. It wasn't unusual for an enquiry to take two years to process – by which time it was no longer relevant."

The ministry was performing so badly that no one cared what anyone else was doing, and unproductive employees flew under the radar for the first couple of years. "We kept the door shut for a while, turned it all inside out, then reopened. By that time, we were performing so well that no one dared interfere. Anyway, we were already too far down the rabbit hole of change." Van Massenhove had a clear vision: to create a place where he himself would like to work. He wanted a jazzy atmosphere, where employees of all ages would feel at home. But the whole enterprise was aging by the minute. How do you attract fresh talent when you are known as the dullest and worst-performing government service in Belgium?

"Those who applied to us in 2002 did so as a last resort," he admits. "I didn't have a clue how to attract young people, but two were my own children, so I decided to share my problem with them. What would they look for in a modern employer? I soon found out that the younger generation loathes the old-fashioned ways of working. They want to choose where and when to work, and an office environment without prehistoric status symbols, hierarchy and diploma-fetish. It's about trust and being allowed to evaluate your boss. It is about a culture of flexibility."

Suddenly, Van Massenhove gets up, interrupting his story. "More about that later," he says. "I'd like to give you a tour of the building, so you get a better understanding." We wander through the modern, well-furnished office. There are no fixed work stations; instead a variety of silent rooms, flexible workspaces, and meeting places. The floors are connected by large, open staircases and light falls into the building from all angles. On one wall, a quote from René Magritte, expressive because of the way the ministry works: "Freedom is that you can be, not that you have to be." We notice that there is hardly anyone present. "Is it a national holiday?" we ask.

"No, it is just your ordinary working day, but the glue here is trust, and as a leader you must earn it. The more you give, the more you get. Everyone can decide where and when they work. Usually we have around 200 of 1,000 civil servants present." Moments later, a child runs by and a staff member proudly tells us that it is her grandchild. "Her parents had to work," she says, "so I decided to bring her in. She's followed the cleaners around and now we're off to the park."

We kept the door
shut for a while,
turned it all inside
out, then reopened.
By that time, we
were performing
so well that no
one dared interfere.
Anyway, we were
already too far down
the rabbit hole
of change.

— Frank van Massenhove

We are beginning to understand why this tour was necessary. There is much to share and be proud of.

We discuss our mutual frustration with traditional structures, wondering why work should still be organised thus. Why is our faith in others so low that we don't trust our colleagues to take the smallest of decisions? Is writing policy manuals really the best use of company time, when they are unlikely to be read? Do we have to impose strict rules on the masses because of the sins of the few?

Many think so. Fear and distrust have a clear playing field. People cling to control systems, even when it has been repeatedly proven that they do not work. In our previous jobs, this drove us mad. The jungle of protocols and control mechanisms, the barrage of rules. It wasn't unusual to spend half our time writing reports for managers so they could feel a sense of control. Unfortunately, the contents (full of quantum chemistry and physics that only true nerds understand) was so arcane that managers could make neither head nor tail of it.

Another example from our past lives: after an employee had been on a business trip, they had to fill out declarations to get their expenses reimbursed. The many pages would have been a challenge for even the most dedicated pencil-pusher. Then the team leader had to approve. After that, the application travelled to a department dedicated to form-checking, day-in and day-out. Most people ended up pushing the limits of what was permissible. A maximum allowance of €300 for hotel accommodation? The bill would come in at €299. Booking a flight that is just within cost limits, but provides you with extra air miles? Go for it! It sounds childish, but that's what happens when you treat people like children.

One of the companies on our Bucket List has a different solution. Streaming movie service Netflix has just one policy when it comes to corporate travel: "Act in Netflix's best interest." Treat company money as if it were your own and make all costs transparent. There is faith that you are responsible enough to make the right decision. The benefit? More autonomy, fewer rules, and no departments needed to do the checking.

The silliness of this system was illustrated by an anecdote from Jean-François Zobrist, former CEO of French manufacturing company FAVI. He spoke with us one Sunday morning at his rural home in northern France. "Once, walking through the factory, I came across Alfred," he said. "He was waiting in front of the storage room and I asked why he was there. He told me: 'I have to change my gloves. I have a coupon from my boss and my old gloves.' The rule was this: when an employee needed new gloves, he had to show the old ones to his boss, take a coupon, go to the storage room, hand in the coupon and the old pair before he was issued with new ones. This process struck me as impractical. The accounting department told me that the machine Alfred operated cost 600 francs per hour to run. Gloves cost about six francs a pair. Do the math. It made me realise that this process was resulting in some very expensive gloves. Even if employees were to take a pair home from time-to-time, everyone would win."

The irony is grim. Many pioneers agree that only three percent of the workforce is likely to take advantage of the system. This means that rules are implemented to keep this rogue three percent in line, which stifles the productivity, autonomy and joy of the 97 percent. A lack of trust in employees and colleagues, plus the need to have an illusion of control, equals a loss of autonomy.

Our modern way of working makes people ill. A recent study by TNO (Netherlands Organisation for Applied Scientific Research) found a growing problem of burnout[28]. One of the main reasons is a decrease in autonomy: people feel they have too little control over what happens in their workday – and the situation is getting worse. It seems we're going back to the industrial era.

Conclusion? It doesn't look good for freedom and trust in the workplace. We see mental and physical health complaints, discontent, and poor motivation – and how enormous the gap between knowing and doing. Research consistently shows the benefits of autonomy, freedom, and trust – yet nothing changes.

HAPPY CIVIL SERVANTS

Frank van Massenhove tells us of the challenges he faced. "The goal was to make civil servants happy and create a more efficient government. The ministry wants to be an attractive place where customers and employees feel at home." This provided the starting point, shared the vision and gave staff an important role in the process. "We told our people: 'This is our destination, but how we get there is up to you'." The message was clear. "To say our goodbyes to the beast, we had to do things differently and question all practices and assumptions. We wanted to reinvent and rebuild. We asked ourselves what people really wanted." The ministry posed some tricky questions, such as: How would we design this from scratch? How do we build a government department aimed at customer satisfaction and results-driven work, where the employees are happy?

"During this three-year-transformation, we tried to involve the civil servants as much as possible. To change a corporate culture, it's important to have the employees on your side." How does that work in practice? By having the employees describe their ideal future. By maintaining connection with them, getting information and learning from it. Leaders ask what bothers people, what drives them, and what changes would make them happy[29].

Employees
their time at
for the sake
This became

a perverse
who could
longest.

were spending
the office
of it.
competitive,
game to see
stay the

The transformation was mainly thought-out by the civil servants via responses to questions. Van Massenhove admits he didn't come up with many new ideas. "Most of it was thought up by our people. We visited all manner of companies and government offices... and then stole their ideas[29]."

Civil servants are given the freedom to decide how the service can best be renewed. Employees are capable of contributing to change and their views should be taken seriously. Civil servants know the ins and outs of the government better than anyone, and they drove this transformation. The first steps were taken, and the obsession with time was replaced by a focus on results. "It makes no sense to check the number of hours people spend behind their desks and not to care whether they deliver. It is often assumed that people are productive when they sit behind their desks." Employees were spending their time at the office for the sake of it. This became competitive, a perverse game to see who could stay the longest. Going home before your boss was not done. This had to change. "We wanted to focus on results."

The ministry now operates in the network-of-teams structure, with the groups evaluating their representative; status symbols are things of the past. Senior management sits at the same table as the others. Ministry staff have complete freedom to design their working day: on average, only six hours – but they are far more productive. During the first three years, productivity rose by 18 percent, and after that by an average of 10 percent per year. The ministry has the lowest number of illness-related absences in Belgium, and there is virtually no burnout. It won the Gender Balanced Organisation Award (without a gender policy in place) and in each department, the sexes are equally represented. Frank credits this to flexibility: "Others have a lot of women working part-time, to balance work and home life. There is no need for that here."

The ministry managed to create an environment that attracts fresh talent. "Before the transformation, we received, on average, three applications for each vacancy. Now we are looking at close to 60." In the bad old days, only 18 percent of civil service applicants wanted to work here; that percentage has risen to 93. "We provide evidence that a culture based on freedom and trust really does work. We do the same work, but the way we do it is different." Is this newer system only of interest to the younger generation? Van Massenhove thinks not. "We aim at them, but who is happier? The older generation. I'll show you how we practise freedom and trust." We walk past a closed door, where Frank stops and smiles. "We allow employees to decorate their workspace," he laughs, as he opens the door. "This is our IT department's choice: a room with no natural light, full of glaring screens!"

The ministry shows how work can be radically different and better. There really are places where people flourish. Work becomes more pleasant and results improve. Of course, it is not easy to make this work from day one; it is a difficult process, but worth the effort. You need more than a conviction that things can be different: you need a healthy dose of grit. Van Massenhove demonstrated this by initially keeping quiet and forging ahead. If the ministers had been aware of his plan, they would have put a stop to it. "Never in my life have I encountered people as risk-averse as politicians. Everyone wants an efficient, unchanging government. So, I kept my mouth shut until we achieved the necessary results." A true rebel at work.

Was it important to have the physical presence of a civil servant at the ministry, five days a week? Very soon, it became clear that the answer was no. Once that was accepted and understood, the challenge was to ensure that the civil servants newly liberated from the office could operate efficiently at a distance. For staff who work remotely, the first item on the management agenda is to have a proper

IT setup. All team members – civil servants in this case – receive a laptop and telephone with internet access. As soon as this infrastructure is in place, there is freedom and flexibility to work – at the office, from a hotel room, from a café, or from home. Current technology enables this – so why not use it?

But those are not the only changes in the ministry's case. The clocking-in system was abolished, processes became more user-friendly, the workplace became more pleasant, files were digitalised. There was no need for civil servants to come to the office and delve into filing cabinets. They regained control of their lives. "Of the 92 percent of civil servants who can freely 'roam', around 69 percent prefer to work mainly from home," Frank says. "The remainder come to the office as usual. Those who want to know how many hours they work can keep track. A few – maybe 16 percent – still do, and I'm fine with that. Many come to the office because it is a nice place to work and to meet up. But as I said, we don't check their hours, we focus on results."

The free-range civil servants are encouraged to come in once a fortnight at a day and time chosen by team members. The most important point, as always, is that employees have the freedom to decide for themselves. You might be wondering how this applies to organisations that are bound to their place of work, such as factory workers, retail staff and care assistants. Even here we have seen that employees who are responsible for their own results are smart enough to know where they need to be, and when. Rules are not necessary. Give choice and responsibility to the teams, not the bureaucrats.

The civil servants of the Belgian Ministry of Social Security prove that it is nonsense to insist that employees work from 9 to 5 without considering productivity. The other extreme of the uninspiring workplace is the desire to have employees working, or thinking about work, 24/7. In many sectors, an 80-hour working week is a must for

We wanted an
office where
everyone, from
founder to secretary,
would have their say.
We wanted everyone
to feel, and act,
like an
entrepreneur.

— Sjoerd van der Velden

a successful career. Whether explicitly or implicitly, you are always deemed to be available. This diseased culture is to be found in many places. One is the legal profession.

Fortunately, even here, there are firms that side-step the rat race. We got to know two of them on opposite sides of the world. In New Zealand, we visited Wellington-based WCLC, where a hierarchical pyramid was dismantled over six months. This firm introduced transparency and dispensed with many unnecessary processes. In Europe, we paid our respects to another progressive law firm, Brugging & Van der Velden in Utrecht. BvdV was founded in 2006 and is known for its four-day working week; employees are discouraged from working longer. We met one of the founders, Sjoerd van der Velden.

EVERYONE IS EQUAL

We were expecting a stuffy office filled with people in suits. Not at all; he welcomes us in jeans and a jumper. He is accompanied by one of his younger colleagues, Martina. "This is so you're not just hearing from me," he says. "Martina's way more capable of explaining how we work, and she'll keep me on track." A wonderful start; we can't wait for the rest of the day.

They take us to a large meeting room where we take a seat at an oval table, enjoying a couple of typically Dutch slices of bread with hagelslag (chocolate sprinkles – if you haven't tried it, you should). Van der Velden brings the coffee and pours milk, the first sign that everyone is equal here. Over lunch, he tells us that he is inspired by the ideas of Brazilian entrepreneur and Bucket List pioneer Ricardo Semler. "For years I worked for one of the more traditional law firms," he says. "I wasn't particularly unhappy, but always knew that, even in our line of work, things could be done in a different way. I am referring to some of the adverse effects of the traditional partner structure: the strict hierarchy, the ridiculous working hours and the limited possibilities for growth. Semler showed that employees perform better when they have freedom and trust. Why wouldn't you give this to them? In 2006, we used this as a basis for setting up the firm. We wanted an office where everyone, from founder to secretary, would have their say. We wanted everyone to feel, and act, like an entrepreneur. The place should belong to everyone."

This office has some 20 employees, a number deliberately kept low – but everyone has a say. Important decisions are taken during six-monthly meetings, at this table. All matters that touch on the philosophy of the business are discussed, and everyone is expected to contribute. The meetings are never chaired by the same person and the participants don't seek a democratic majority but strive for consensus. Equality is paramount. That is not all that sets BvdV apart. Unlike traditional firms – where a person who brings in more work receives a bigger slice of the pie – equity partner appointments here must be agreed upon by all employees. "We take more social requirements into account. The shares staff receive give them the right to dividends only while they are in their possession and for a maximum of 13 years. This ensures that there are always chances for promotion, even if you joined quite recently."

But how does BvdV break with the most stubborn vice of law firms: the oppressive working week? Martina explains: "Everyone is personally responsible for the number of hours they work. There is so much trust that we can decide how many days we work, how many hours we work, and what our hourly rate is. We don't keep track of annual leave. Are you on holiday? If so, you don't bill hours." This isn't without obligation. "Freedom and responsibility go hand-in-hand. We work with what we call a break-even point (BEP). Each year, we calculate how many billable hours should be put in to keep the place running. Beyond that point, every hour is profit. Everyone receives a basic salary, but also benefits from hours that exceed the BEP." It is in everybody's interest to keep costs down. The sooner the BEP is reached, the higher the shared profit. Everyone benefits and employees' interest runs parallel with that of the office. It ensures that everyone acts responsibly and there is no excessive spending. Administration – answering of phones, photocopying, clearing desks, making coffee and dishwasher duties – are shared tasks.

It leaves the most important question unanswered: how does BvdV ensure that people don't just focus on making as much money as possible? "There is a yearly maximum, equivalent to about 1,128 billable hours (six hours a day, four days a week, 47 weeks a year) that you can make at the firm," says Martina. "We introduced a turnover cap instead of turnover targets to prevent over-billing and introduced the four-day week. Sure, you can work more hours, but it isn't financially beneficial. We believe that a healthy work-life balance is essential for creativity and long-term employment. A working week of four days is the norm, not the exception."

Let's take a look at the "normal" working week. In a 9-to-5 day, how do you set your goals, measure what you have achieved or quantify your progress? By working in teams, and making the whole team responsible for results, you replace top-down control with a form of peer review. You and your colleagues are keeping tabs on performance; this is different to being accountable to a boss. How results are measured depends on the team. For some, this is the number of parts manufactured or response time, for others it's the level of customer satisfaction (or the number of complaints received). It is easy to see what the liberal process has given BvdV in return. And there are other places where flexibility ensures a better work-life balance.

FOUR DAYS WORKS FINE

One is to be found in New Zealand. Asset management firm Perpetual Guardian experimented for two months with a four-day work week for its 240 employees. The workers were still paid for five days, and the trial was evaluated by the Auckland University of Technology. The result? Seventy-eight percent of employees were happy with the integration of their working and private lives, and stress levels reduced[30]. Motivation and performance increased.

It often happens that people hear these success stories, and immediately assume that this should be the new norm. Resist the urge. The most important thing is to establish what does and does not work. One thing we have learned, is that there is no holy grail, no silver bullet, no one-size-fits-all. The point is that every organisation should dare to experiment to gain new insights and see if there is a better way.

We introduced a turnover cap instead of turnover targets to prevent over-billing and introduced the four-day week. Sure, you can work more hours, but it isn't financially beneficial.

— Martina van Eldik

The four-day week may be the answer to one of the problems occasionally thrown-up by flexible working hours: having no one around when staff are suddenly – sometimes desperately –needed. Here's a solution from Kath Blackham, who founded VERSA in Melbourne 10 years ago. VERSA employs 55 people and its purpose is "making people's lives better" via web, mobile and platform development, including voice technology. The firm is a serial award-winner, with half its customer base composed of non-profits and government organisations. We meet Blackham on her home turf to discuss the implications of a shorter week.

Since 2018, VERSA employees have been packing their hours into just four working days. Blackham had to fight to ring in the new schedule, but she persisted: reducing hours in industries where long days are the norm has been shown to be beneficial. "For the employees," Blackham says, "(the extra day off) could boost mental health, allow time for parenting, and encourage entrepreneurship. There are benefits for business too, such as more focused work, less absenteeism and higher productivity."

Blackham pitched the idea to the rest of the leadership team, initially to no avail; there were fears that revenues may drop. She refused to take no for an answer – and set up an experiment. For 90 days, three staff members shoe-horned their usual hours into a four-day week; they were paid for five. In terms of billable hours, profit and revenues, the results were overwhelmingly positive. The experiment was swiftly extended to include all employees. Creative director Andrew Isaac reflects: "It was hard early on, and everyone had to find their own way. I had to figure out how to schedule all my meetings and still be productive. That wasn't easy, but it has certainly helped me to work smarter. I feel it was the same for the others."

After a year, it was clear to Blackham and her colleagues that the right move had been made. "Profits have doubled, revenue has grown by 46 percent, and staff retention has gone from 77 percent to 88. People are healthier, happier, and less likely to take sick days." Blackham is nonetheless reluctant to give the quart-in-a-pint-pot schedule all the credit. "It's hard to say how much of our progress can be attributed to the four-day work week," she admits, "but it was a success that can't be denied."

PIONEERING PRACTICES FROM AROUND THE GLOBE

The Belgian ministry, Dutch law firm BvdV and VERSA are great examples of progressives that organise themselves according to freedom and trust. They replace old-fashioned management theories with new ideas, liberate themselves from rules and checks, and respect their employees. And they reap wonderful rewards.

Disclaimer: This does not mean that everyone does whatever they want. When nobody looks at the hours you work, only results, you must deliver. When control mechanisms go, you can't hide behind the rules. You will have to use your own judgement. Progressives want you to make full use of your brain and work autonomously. Traditional management is replaced by common sense and a compassionate, inclusive agenda. We have some ideas to inspire you ...

VEL 1 DESIGN YOUR OWN WORKPLACE

Empower employees: give them the freedom to design and decorate. It's a simple way to provide the first level of autonomy. Let them decide what they need; often this is down to a variety of spaces: silent places, meeting rooms, and a comfortable spot for relaxation. Think back to the IT team at the Belgian ministry. Some people need an open space, others prefer an office without windows. Provided the choice lies with the employees, you're always doing the right thing.

VEL 2 RESULTS-BASED WORKING

If you judge employees by results, you should work in a result-orientated manner. How to set and reach targets, how to measure performance – these metrics vary. Some decide team goals on a weekly basis and make this visible on a wall or whiteboard – or use an online tool, such as Trello. It's all about being able to evaluate progress. How the employees manage this is their own affair. This results-orientated way of working is a boost for motivation and ensures that employees contribute.

VEL 3 REMOVE CONTROL MECHANISMS

Chuck the time-clock out of a top-floor window, forget fixed working hours, give your employees freedom. Provide unlimited holidays, burn those fat folders of policy documentation, stop creating rules for the three percenters, and encourage common sense. If you don't trust your employees, why did you hire them in the first place? Does everything go wrong when you show trust? Are people not turning up for work? If so, perhaps there is no fire in their bellies. If, on the other hand, no one is taking their annual leave, you have a whole other issue to sort out (and this happens surprisingly often). Address the cause of problems, not the symptoms. Provide freedom and trust and start doing the real work.

It isn't exactly breaking news that traditional companies are like sloths on downers when it comes to decision-making. Processes are cumbersome and lead to more bottlenecks than you'd find in a brewery.

LEVEL 4 PEER REVIEW

Top-down control and reviews are standard in most traditional companies. Cut it out! It serves nobody. Progressives show there's another way. Let workers be accountable to their colleagues, not to the boss. Create an environment where this is possible. Learn how to provide valid, regular feedback. Create a culture of transparency,

LEVEL 5 SELF-SETTING SALARIES

The true radicals allow workers the freedom to determine their own pay level. Various companies are doing this – and it works. Traditionally, salary setting is accompanied by secrets, gossip, politics, and dishonesty. The result is an often-uneasy consensus. At progressive places, people are forced to think about real added value. They know that after setting their own goals and evaluating themselves, determining their own pay is the next step.

CHAPTER 6

FROM CENTRALISED TO DISTRIBUTED AUTHORITY

Towards the end of the 1990s, American Navy submarine commander David Marquet made the decision to give as few orders as possible. His approach was as determined as it was radical, and he followed through, making just a tiny percentage of decisions on board the nuclear-powered vessel. One might have expected such a move to result in chaos, and potentially dangerous chaos at that. Instead came some fascinating developments. Marquet's submarine became more functional, with his crew performing better than ever. Few would have expected that such a radical delegation of authority would prove successful within the rigid hierarchy of the military — or that it would even be possible. How did the commander pull this off, and what can we learn from it? Time for a Corporate Rebels investigation...

When we got in touch with Marquet, he informed us that he would soon be sharing his story at a Danish convention. It didn't take much time for us to decide that we were going to tag along, and once again we found ourselves on a plane, this time bound for Copenhagen. The plan was to kill a few birds with the same stone and use the trip to carry out other Bucket List investigations. We would spend some time with Alexander Kjerulf, author of Happy Hour is 9-to-5, and Lars Kolind, the former CEO of hearing aid manufacturer Oticon. Kolind is another pioneer of note who broke with workplace tradition.

KEYS TO THE SUB

We arrive in Copenhagen on a sunny Spring day. We quickly spot Marquet, casually attired in jeans, blue shirt and black jacket. Not exactly the dress code we would have expected from a former navy commander, but the intensity of his gaze lets you know you're dealing with a military man, and a mariner. On stage at the event, Marquet shares his special approach — described in his autobiographical book Turn The Ship Around: A True Story of Turning Followers into Leaders[31]. During the presentation, and later in conversation, he makes it clear that his breakthrough was (as so often) born of necessity, and not a tale of sunshine and rainbows.

"When I was a young man, I decided I was going to be the captain of a nuclear submarine," he begins, "and I ended up being the captain of ... a nuclear submarine. I was ordered to take command of the USS Olympia, with 135 souls aboard, a vessel able to stay at sea for months at a time." But before he was handed the keys, so to speak, he had to take a year to learn the specifics of the vessel. "I was excited to take command, and I wanted to have a great ship. All I could think of during that year was that I wanted to be able to give great orders to my crew. I thought that if I gave good instructions, I would have a good submarine. If I gave very good instructions, a very good submarine. And if I gave great instructions, I'd have a great submarine. After-all, isn't that what captains of submarines do?"

Studies complete, David Marquet felt well prepared, and couldn't wait. Then he received a phone call from his superiors. "The plan had changed. Just one week before I was scheduled to take command, the Navy said: 'You're not going to the USS Olympia. You're going to the USS Santa Fe.' The previous captain had quit. He'd had enough." So, here was our commander, knowing everything about the Olympia... and almost nothing about the Santa Fe. What little he did know did not inspire him. The Olympia was one of the best vessels in the fleet. The Santa Fe, on the other hand, was the ugly duckling of the US Navy, used as a case study on how not to do things. "The Santa Fe was the sub we all laughed at," says Marquet. "She was the worst performing, with the lowest morale and retention-rate of any submarine. The year before I took command, of the 135 crew members, precisely three had re-enlisted.

"I was not happy. I was petrified, because I was trained for the Olympia and the Santa Fe was a very different submarine. My technical knowledge wasn't necessarily going to apply. I tried to picture myself aboard the Santa Fe giving all those great instructions. How was I going to do that if I didn't know anything about the vessel?" When he first set foot on the Santa Fe, it was obvious that crew morale was at a low ebb. "I'm the new boss and I'm walking through," he recalls. "The passageways are narrow, like on an airplane. I'm bumping into people, and would say: 'How are you?' And they were like zombies. They'd been beaten down because they had made mistakes. Control had been taken away from them — and they made more mistakes. The crew were thinking: 'Oh please, just let me get through the day'."

The new commander had his own worries. "Now remember, they've just sent me to the worst-performing sub – and I had an inspection coming up. "I was going to sea for a week, we were going to fire torpedoes, there was going to be a complement of senior officers watching every move. I told my crew to study the book, study the book, study the book. With so little time, we had a lot to do." While in the engine room, Marquet noticed a pump sitting in the middle of the deck. There was no one in sight. "That pump needed to be installed and functional. I found the chief of the machinery department, and asked: 'What's going on? Why isn't that pump being fixed?' He said: 'Well, Captain, they didn't order the right part.' I asked: 'They? Who's they?' He answered: 'The supply department'.

"Now, on a submarine, the supply department chief sleeps directly above the machinery department chief." It was a textbook example of where central decision-making can lead. Employees stop using their common sense and simply await orders. It is not particularly surprising to see this in the Navy. The crew is expected to carry out commands, not question them. This doesn't apply just to the military. Most traditional organisations operate via a centralised decision-making process, with power mainly in the hands of the elite few. The higher up the pyramid you are, the more clout you have. Decisions flow through the layers in the hope that employees will carry out orders as precisely as possible — whether they agree with them or not. If the employees come up with ideas, they will seek approval before taking any action.

A century ago, centralising decision-making was a sound idea. It was the way to co-ordinate matters, to ensure that decision-makers were well informed, and that the decisions dovetailed with strategy. It was sensible in an unchanging world. Education levels were lower, policies more pragmatic and linear. But those days are behind us. Today, employees usually do have a good educational background, and are capable of adapting. It's no longer acceptable to sit on your hands, waiting for someone "upstairs" to make the decision. Centralisation simply doesn't mesh with modern ways and circumstances.

This is something that we experienced frequently before the birth of Corporate Rebels. Here is one painful example: When putting together a proposal for major clients, signatures had to be collected. The first step was to visit all the managers who had to sign. The questions posed by them weren't related to content; this was an ass-covering exercise. No one had a clue what was going on at the front line. Cheques were written by those in the ivory tower. The first signatory bore the brunt of responsibility by virtue of origination. If something went wrong, that person was to blame. It was a huge relief as soon as that first signature was obtained, but it carried on. Responsibility, ownership, and entrepreneurship were irrelevant. Those at the top carried a responsibility for things they knew nothing about.

The result of centralised decision-making is frustration, an unwillingness to take responsibility, inertia, poor choices and endless "co-ordination". This frustration is borne by all. To have everything you do verified, approved, and signed-off means that somewhere along the line, the system is broken. It isn't exactly breaking news that traditional companies are like sloths on downers when it comes to decision-making. Processes are cumbersome and lead to more bottlenecks than you'd find in a brewery. Studies show that delays in decision-making result in one-third of all products being delivered late or incomplete[32]. A good deal of time at work is spent waiting. If all this waiting resulted in great outcomes, it wouldn't be so bad. But that is not the case.

Traditional companies are not just slow in decision-making, they're also bad at it. A survey by McKinsey found that 72 percent of senior executives felt that bad decisions were made as frequently as good ones or were "the prevailing norm"[33]. Ouch.

LIVING IN THE PAST

We often live in the past, with structures and processes that were designed for a world that no longer exists. It's like playing the latest Rockstar game on a Nokia 3310. This is the reason progressives delegate. Imagine how it would feel to be autonomous. It would increase your engagement. If companies were to treat their employees as responsible adults, what would the workplace look like? Those questions were answered for us in Copenhagen by David Marquet.

"We were preparing for the inspection," Marquet continues. "Now remember, even though I was trained for the other submarine, I was familiar with giving orders and instructions. That is what captains do. I would give an order — well, more of a suggestion — to the officer of the deck. Then one of the junior sailors, the person who was supposed to do the job, would say: 'We can't do that.' On this submarine, unlike all the others I had been on, it seemed impossible for anyone to carry out an order. It just didn't make any sense."

Once aboard, the crew accepted orders without question, even if they couldn't be carried out. Marquet knew that change had to come, and quickly. But he also knew that as commanding officer, he was part of the problem. He saw that he had to alter the top-down leadership style. Instead of giving more "impossible" orders, he started roaming his sub and quizzing the crew about anything and everything. What would you do if you were in my shoes? What works well on the Santa Fe? What are your biggest frustrations? Why is the submarine performing so badly? What do you hope I will change? What things do you want to keep the same? What is the best I can do for you? How can I help you to perform better?[31]

Marquet discovered the good and the bad. He soon found out that the old way of getting things done was frustrating. His new approach was in the style of Ari Weinzweig in Ann Arbor, pouring water for the guests in his restaurant: management by wandering around. That's a term thought-up by American management-guru Tom Peters. Peters, also one of our Bucket List pioneers, enlightened us. The most important thing in these random sorties, Peters told us, is spontaneity.

When we blogged about the "Iceberg of Ignorance"[36], that post went viral. This legend originated (it's said) in 1989, when consultant Sidney Yoshida produced a study on the leadership habits of Japanese car manufacturer, Calsonic. Yoshida uncovered poor distribution of power and information. Specifically, knowledge of front-line problems declined the higher it climbed the management chain. He found that even though all those problems were known to the front-line employees, only 74 percent of team leaders, nine percent of middle-management and just four percent of top brass were aware of them. Whether Yoshida's numbers are accurate and relevant today is debatable, but with inexplicable behaviour in the workplace, there will be room for this speculation. The Iceberg is a fine analogy of the miserable state of the modern workplace. In good times, this situation may not be crucial. But in bad times, leaders need urgent and accurate information to survive. This is when roles are suddenly reversed. Leaders with low status and trust can end up feeling like Julius Caesar on the Ides of March. They will be left to solve their problems in isolation. Obviously, it is impossible for even the most heroic leadership team to solve all problems, especially if they are only aware of the tip of the iceberg.

The problem doesn't only occur top-to-bottom. The challenges known to top management are often widely misunderstood by front-line staff – the perfect ingredients for miscommunication, misunderstanding and misjudgement. During his managing-by-walking-around phase, the commander would ask crew members what their specific task was. "Whatever they tell me to do," was the most common reply. It spoke volumes. This not only characterised the crew's sheep-like

It's no longer acceptable to sit on your hands, waiting for someone "upstairs" to make the decision. Centralisation simply doesn't mesh with modern ways and circumstances.

mentality but also highlighted the biggest potential danger of traditional workplace cultures. Of the 135 members of Marquet's crew, only five — all officers — knew anything about the work to be done. The others were just following orders and had their brains on standby. "The more we take control, the less people think," he says. "As I was trained for another submarine, I really needed my people to think. I had to stop taking control. I said: 'Look, I'm not going to give any more orders, because when I give an order you follow it. If I give the wrong order, we're all going to die.' It changed the entire culture. We went from one person telling 134 people what to do to 135 people – creative, proactive people – who were actively thinking."

The crew were rewarded with more control. Marquet increased motivation and decreased bureaucracy. He no longer handed out specific tasks but provided guidelines. He ensured that the officers created task lists. He resolved only to ask questions that would reveal how crew members could solve their own problems. Marquet decided to build on this, and step-by-step freed the USS Santa Fe from control mechanisms and the directive style of leadership that is so typical of the Navy. He abolished top-down control and delegated decision-making as much as possible. "Don't move information to authority, move authority to information," he wrote in *Turn The Ship Around*.

After his first three weeks on the Santa Fe, it was time for the dreaded inspection. "They boarded the submarine and ... suddenly all these strange things happened. The exercises went well. People were thinking for themselves, not waiting to be told what to do. They loaded the torpedo right. We didn't make the usual mistakes. It was as if everyone had somehow become smarter. I couldn't understand it; this was exactly 21 days since I stepped aboard.

"My boss said: 'It's a new submarine.' He gave us a grade that took us from the bottom of the fleet to halfway up the rankings. It was astounding. I told the officers that I wasn't going to be in control and gave them authority. They began to understand that we were in this as a team. What we did was make people happier. There was no way we could have learned what we needed to know in such a short time. But you can make people happier in that timeframe. When people are happier, they don't just act smarter, they are smarter. We made people happy first and performance followed."

This is an American story, so we now need the happy ending. Within a year, the USS Santa Fe went from the worst performing submarine in the fleet to the best. The happiest part of this happy ending is that Marquet's influence remained strong, long after he had moved on. "We know what happens when we give people control," he says. "They participate, becoming passionate and energised. They start using their brains. They come up with ideas. The next year it wasn't three mariners who re-enlisted, it was 33. We created 10 commanding officers from one crew, a highly disproportionate number."

David Marquet showed that employees taking important decisions have a greater sense of entrepreneurship and pride. They start thinking for themselves. People in the front line know what the issues are, how to solve them, and how to make the lives of customers and suppliers easier. It becomes possible to free-up time for leaders that are no longer creating bottlenecks.

In traditional organisations, we see two decision-making methods. The first and the most popular is the directive top-down style that David Marquet learned, then learned to avoid. Leaders dominate by telling their teams how to implement instructions. At the other end of the spectrum is the consensus method. Both options are familiar and have their pros and cons. Progressives have said goodbye to these stereotypes and adopted alternative strategies. Commander Marquet demonstrated how the process can be better distributed

I'm not
going to give
any more orders,
because when
I give an order
you follow it.
If I give
the wrong order,
we're all going
to die.

— David Marquet

without messing with hierarchy. And we have encountered other interesting initiatives, where leaders situate decision-making authority as low as possible.

To prevent the walking-through-treacle syndrome, and drowning in sluggish processes based on consensus, many progressives apply another approach: the advice process. We were introduced to this practice over dinner with Frederic Laloux, the author of the highly popular (rightly so) book *Reinventing Organisations*. Later, we saw the advice process in action at the Brazilian IT company Vagas, with the British developers of Smarkets, and the American tomato-processors at Morning Star.

Doug Kirkpatrick and Paul Green Jnr, both early employees of Morning Star, told us more about this during our visits to the factory in Los Gatos, California. "The main concept is relatively simple," said Kirkpatrick. "If properly implemented, it is incredibly effective. It allows everyone to take a certain amount of authority and make decisions.

"There is one qualification: before anyone makes a decision, they must seek appropriate advice. This has to be given by people who will be affected by the decision, and who have relevant experience. Different perspectives will be considered, but in the end it is up to the decision-maker to say what is needed. Advice is just advice."

The process leaves responsibility with the decision-maker; there is no need for an authority figure. This makes the strategy effective and sturdy. It allows each employee to develop initiatives and take the reins without frustrating compromises. The most important thing is that employees take ownership of decisions that affect them.

We are regularly invited to share knowledge we have gleaned at conferences and congresses; frequently we are invited to visit companies to talk about pioneers we have met. These are good moments for us to learn about potential new Bucket List destinations. The truly radical examples remain elusive. In Barcelona, where we gave a presentation to the board of a large fashion company, we received a tip about a fresh pioneering firm with a style of its own.

It will come as no surprise, dear reader, to learn that soon after getting wind of this, we were sitting in a plane. And on a cold November day we arrived at the small Swiss mountain town of Sankt Gallen to visit the head office of HR software company Haufe-Umantis...

EMPLOYEES IN THE LEAD

The view is breathtaking, a bright blue sky and snowy streets. We are enjoying a warming cup of coffee at the company's in-house bar. The CEO is Marc Stoffel, a jovial and enthusiastic man who is the only democratically chosen chief executive we have come across. He has three-day stubble, a blue shirt and dark jeans. Stoffel gives us the tour of the modern building: bright colours, a lot of glass, and a back wall papered with Polaroids of company staff. We take our seats and get down to business.

We start with the company's founding. "In 2001," Stoffel begins, "Hermann Arnold decided to set up Umantis with the goal of fixing the traditional way of working." Arnold was heavily influenced by democratic ideals and built Umantis accordingly. His mantra: "Employees should lead companies." Hermann Arnold's words still influence how people treat one another and how the company does business. "It is our mission to allow employees to lead to the best of their abilities." This company has more in common with a democratic micronation than your average commercial enterprise.

The democratic journey of discovery led to some surprising destinations. When Stoffel joined in 2005, there were 20 employees. "The first real democratic decision was taken in 2008," he tells us. The company was in dire financial straits. Necessity seems so often the catalyst for change... Drastic action had to be taken. Arnold called a meeting of all 70 employees and explained the situation. He provided two options that could ensure survival. Either he would start firing, or they could all take a pay cut. Managers would sacrifice 30 percent of their pay, while employees would drop by 15 percent. Over 90 percent of workers supported the cuts – and that's the path he took.

WISDOM OF THE CROWD

It sounds more like new-age mumbo-jumbo than ancient Greek philosophical wisdom. The concept of crowd wisdom, however, goes back that far. It was Aristotle who found that a big crowd is smarter than a few experts.

In 1906, a researcher named Francis Galton canvassed 800 people at a country fair. He asked them to estimate the weight of a slaughtered ox. Galton found that the average estimate of 1207 pounds was accurate to within one percent[34]. A more recent example is Wikipedia. Many claimed that the site could not be trusted because of its anonymous contributors – but that proved not to be the case. The science journal *Nature* says the open-access site is about as accurate as the old and much respected *Encyclopaedia Britannica*[35].

We are all familiar with the concept of the wisdom of the crowd without realising it. Most of us use it frequently in our private lives, such as when asking support on online forums or social media. Nevertheless, many traditional organisations ignore this. They even give those at the top the monopoly on most decisions. Unfortunately, decisions are then made on the basis of corporate systems and formal reports. This means they often miss out on relevant information. This is a shame, because it ignores so much latent knowledge.

Democratic decisions worked so well for Haufe-Umantis that nowadays this is the norm. Marc Stoffel says the collective process has many benefits. "Firstly, it offers employees clarity on the most important decisions," he tells us. "It ensures that all are aware of the key events. Employees study the situation and pose queries before they make judgement calls. Because they are actively involved, they are usually able to accept any outcome. We vote to follow a certain direction and are naturally motivated to ensure that it works. This is a good exercise to see whether management understands the reality of the front line."

That first successful experiment inspired Haufe-Umantis to set up a new one in 2012. Arnold came to think that he was no longer the most suitable person to fill the chief executive role. The company had seen rapid growth and he thought it was time for a fresh hand on the tiller. A CEO with a different set of leadership qualities would be a better fit. He decided to step down, and rather than simply appointing a replacement, he asked himself a fundamental question. Why shouldn't employees choose their own leader? "I'm sure you've guessed it," smiled Stoffel. Herman Arnold called for another staff meeting. By this time, the company had about 100 employees. Arnold shared his ideas. "This is where we are," he told the workers, "so let's take a vote." And they did.

"That was when I became the first democratically chosen CEO of Haufe-Umantis," Stoffel says, "with 95 percent of the vote. Not a bad score, if I say so myself!" The experiment had unexpected consequences for the other board members. "They also wanted to be democratically selected," Stoffel says. "I asked them if they were sure, because I suspected that some would be voted out." The board stuck to their guns. "This was the first major leadership clean-out. I had warned them of the possible consequences, and it became bitter reality for some. One board member had 100 percent against him. That must have been incredibly painful."

It was clear: there was no room for poor leadership. "The mood was tense," Stoffel recalls, "and some of the former board members needed time to reflect. But I am glad to say that all those who were voted out are either still with the company or left for other reasons – and without any hard feelings."

The experiments show the true democratic nature of this company. This way of working is suitable for the people involved and given the relatively small size of the company. "I have been chosen as CEO for the last four-and-a-half years," says Stoffel, "but at the last election I received only 68 percent of the votes, and I needed 66. We'll have to wait and see what the next elections will bring."

PIONEERING PRACTICES FROM AROUND THE GLOBE

An important feature of traditional organisations is central authority. This implies that decision-making competence rises according to one's position in the hierarchy, but the claim is complete nonsense. Progressives tend to be decentralised. The crew of the USS Santa Fe and democratic Haufe-Umantis show that decision-making can be spread throughout the organisation, resulting in higher productivity and better decision-making.

Many progressive organisations continuously adapt to a rapidly changing work environment. They understand that centralised decision-making processes cause the organisation to be slow-footed. That is why they often rely on the individuals and teams closest to the front line. These employees know the customers, suppliers and facilities best, and must take the lion's share of the decisions. Distributed authority and decision-making processes are trending, but don't relax too soon: the freedom to take decisions is accompanied by responsibility.

So, how can you start? This is what some of the pioneers do.

LEVEL 1 MAP DECISION-MAKING

Teams may not know if they're allowed to take a certain decision. Leaders may struggle to let go of authority. Many solve this with a simple first step. They map the current situation and provide an overview of who does what. If you don't over-complicate things, this can be fixed in a single morning. Don't worry about questions that arise once in a blue moon, just consider the basics. The rest will follow.

How do you go about doing this as a team? Simple: gather your colleagues and clarify who makes which decisions. Discuss whether this makes sense. We see the following divisions within many progressive companies:

> Simple decisions: just do it. Progressives believe it's better to ask forgiveness rather than permission
> Medium to big decisions: Advice process

Make sure that this overview of decision-making is visible afterwards, so that everyone knows where they stand. We want to prevent further chaos!

LEVEL 2 CHANGE THE LANGUAGE

David Marquet on the USS Santa Fe changed the language of the organisation and showed that this can be a powerful step towards distributed decision-making. Try to replace passive phrases with ones that imply initiative and ownership.

Managers can also change their language. Instead of giving answers, they should be asking questions. When employees ask for permission or approval, simply ask "What do you propose?". A great and simple way to distribute decision-making.

LEVEL 3 PUSH AUTHORITY DOWN

Once it is clear who makes the decisions it's time to distribute authority down the chain of command. Ensure that everyone seeks out practices that hold people back. Search for pesky mechanisms that keep the command-and-control culture in place. For example: managers who have to sign-off on travel expenses or approve working from home. You can also follow the steps of another of David Marquet's best practices (which we adapt slightly):

> Sit down with your team and map the decision-making (see point 1)
> Team member(s) identify decisions they want to take by them selves.
> Let leaders express any concerns. If they feel some people cannot or should not make certain decisions, this is the time to say why.
> Together alleviate the concerns as much as possible. Train, educate, or inform people so that they can make the decisions. It's about pushing decision-making down.

The first step in changing the genetic code of any organisation or system is delegating control, or decision-making authority, as much as is comfortable, and then adding a pinch more. This isn't an empowerment programme. It's changing the way the organisation controls decisions in an enduring, personal way.

LEVEL 4 PRE-APPROVAL

Henry Stewart, CEO of the British training bureau Happy, introduced us to another interesting idea: pre-approval. A leader or manager approves something in advance, before the employee has made a decision or found a solution. The approval is given on one condition: adhere to the predefined boundaries. What is the maximum amount of money to be spent? What are its minimum requirements? How much time is allowed? This process allows employees to make their own decisions. Whatever they come up with will be put into practice.

LEVEL 5 ADVICE PROCESS

This is a most radical way of distributing decision-making authority. It provides an alternative to slow consensus and is something we have seen in many organisations. Here's what it looks like:

> Someone takes the initiative to solve a problem
> or grasp an opportunity.
> The decision-maker seeks advice from people
> directly involved and/or more experienced colleagues.
> This advice can be heeded or ignored. The decision-maker
> has the final say.
> The decision-maker ensures that all involved are informed
> about the advice received and the eventual decision.

These steps show clearly that the process is not about reaching a consensus. Not everyone has to agree, not every source has to be taken into account. The decision-maker should get enough advice to make an informed decision.

It sounds more
mumbo-jumbo
Greek
wisdom.
of crowd
however, goes

like new-age
than ancient
philosophical
The concept
wisdom,
back that far.

CHAPTER 7

FROM SECRECY TO RADICAL TRANSPARENCY

From the start, we have been trying to get through the door of the famous pioneer Ricardo Semler. Author of bestseller *Maverick!*, Semler was one of our greatest sources of inspiration, and number one on the Bucket List we compiled way back in 2015 in Barcelona. Unfortunately, that was the easy part; speaking face-to-face to Ricardo Semler proved difficult. Arranging visits to the likes of Google and Haier wasn't a piece of cake, but meeting the Brazilian entrepreneur is on a par with getting a coffee date with Barack Obama. For a long time, our stalking techniques seemed to be getting us nowhere but then, in the summer of 2018, success. In high spirits, we travelled to beautiful Sao Paulo, rented a four-wheel-drive, and set off for a tour of Semco...

Our first port of call is one of Semco's factories in the tiny village of Itatiba, just north of the metropolis. This area used to be rainforest, but the urban sprawl has won out. It has taken an hour to get here, navigating favelas, backroads and rolling hills. We have read so much about this factory and, entering the grounds, it is clear we won't be disappointed. We are welcomed in a colourful relaxation area where employees are chilling in hammocks; no walls interrupt the views of the wooded hillsides. We're here to find out what has become of Semco in the 30 years since the publication of Semler's bestseller. We meet key figures who featured in that story, including former HR director Clovis Bojikian. But it starts, of course, with Ricardo Semler himself.

We meet Semler in a city centre hotel and learn how he transformed the company not once, but twice, to make it one of the World's most progressive businesses. "For me, it all started in 1980 when I was 21 and a law student," he tells us. "I hadn't planned on taking over my father's company – I had different ambitions – but when the opportunity arose, I decided to take it." Antonio Curt Semler, Ricardo's father, was a migrant engineer from Austria who established the business in 1953. At the time of Ricardo's takeover, producing hydraulic pumps as the main export, Antonio Semler led in a traditional way. There was nothing unusual about Semco's operation or management during his time at the helm. It was hierarchical and bureaucratic, and displayed little trust in its employees.

"Just after I took over," says Ricardo, "my dad told me: 'I'm going away for the next two or three weeks. Any changes you want should be implemented while I'm gone.' I took up the challenge and made a list of the top 15 managers. It was a Friday; I made appointments, and by the end of the day, half of them had been fired." Unfortunately, as Semler was to discover, some of those managers were the keepers of company secrets. The consequence was that we spent a lot of time looking for the special deals that managers had made with clients, and we had to dive into the archives. But I don't regret my decision for a moment. We were separating from people who were determined to keep everything to themselves. I didn't know if we were going to survive, but we had to try." Semler is not shy of trial-and-error, and that's how he conducted his quest.

He did not immediately go the progressive route. The transformation that followed the sacking spree was all about "professionalising". (Beware of this term. Although it sounds sensible, it often means control, rules, and bureaucracy.) Dozens of new procedures were implemented in the first two years, and new forms were conceived and printed almost every day. Everything was checked and double-checked. Vendors were obliged to create reports after every visit, employees were randomly searched and made to carry identity cards. It was a false start.

Staff were sceptical of this new, authoritarian approach, and the resulting atmosphere knocked Semler's confidence. He was acutely aware of a lack of staff involvement and engagement. After three years of professionalising, he decided that enough was enough – and hired HR director, Clovis Bojikian. It's here that the story took a turn for the better.

MEETING 'THE 'STACHE'

We meet Bojikian and his wife at their modern apartment in Sao Paolo, the day after our conversation with Semler. The provenance of his nickname – "The 'Stache" – is immediately clear. Clovis has a fine white mustache that Friedrich Nietzsche would have envied. Behind the striking facial hair, we find a kind gentleman. He takes a seat, and his first words set the tone: "You have talked to brilliant and inspiring people before. Now, you meet real people."

Bojikian and Semler were to play pivotal roles in the creation of one of the world's most unusual workplaces: Ricardo as visionary owner, Clovis as pragmatic HR director. It was his job to turn wild ideas and controversial concepts into practical reality. We take our seats and begin to fire off questions. We learn about Bojikian's time before Semco, when he experimented – to mixed results – with alternative ways of working. Recalling the process seems to be a pleasant experience for him as he sinks into storyteller mode.

"When I arrived for my interview, a young chap appeared and took me to a meeting room. I thought he was one of Semco's interns. After I took my seat, he carried on talking. It dawned on me that this was not an intern. It was the man I had come to meet: the owner of the place." He didn't need much time to get over any reservations about Semler's youth. They spent hours scheming and dreaming about how work at Semco could be better organised; they met again the following day. Clovis was appointed somewhere in the midst of these free-flowing discussions, and he plunged right in. He was so excited that it took him a week to realise that one thing he had not discussed with Semler was his salary. That was quickly resolved, and work began in earnest.

Having Bojikian on board facilitated crucial change. To the vision and vigour of Ricardo, he brought experience and pragmatism. They agreed that it was time to stop controlling and regulating everyone and focus on freedom, trust, and openness. The business would be run in a more natural and compassionate way. The more they talked, the more it became obvious that nothing less than a complete overhaul would do the trick. This time there was no fixed plan.

People are
responsible adults
at home. Why do we
suddenly transform
them into
adolescents with
no freedom when
they reach the
workplace?

— Ricardo Semler

"One problem we faced was that in 1984 and 1985 we had acquired four small companies that were even less motivated than our own." With 800 employees, most of them machine operators in five factories, it didn't take long to find a correlation between participation and motivation. But there were no consultants, and no books on how to make such a radical transformation work. "The only way forward was through experimentation. The main question was: How could we improve the daily life of our operators? But we were not going to provide all the answers. We wanted them to participate, to own the problem and the solution."

The first item to be addressed was a seemingly trivial one. At its heart is one of Brazil's most famous dishes — a bean stew called feijoada. People complained about how it was prepared in the works canteen: the beans were too hard, or too soft. Everyone had something to say. It was up to HR to find a solution. "Whatever we proposed, there would still be complaints," he says, "so we turned it back to them and asked: 'What do you suggest?' When they came up with an idea, we asked: 'Is this viable? Did you discuss it with the kitchen staff?' They hadn't, so we sent them off to talk to the cooks; the proposal was tweaked and presented again. 'Great,' we said, 'go ahead and do it. And by the way: you guys are the canteen commission now. We'll have elections every year.' It worked like a charm. The complaining stopped once people had taken ownership of the problem. While the consistency of beans may not seem that important to us, it obviously was to the workers." The episode was a learning experience, a turning point in Semco's transformation.

Another minor issue had to do with company uniforms. Some workers didn't want one; the majority did but couldn't decide on a style or colour. Once again, HR set up a workers' commission. To the question, "Do you want uniforms?", most voted "yes". The next question was: "What colour?" There was no clear winner. The workers' commission added a step to the process and picked the two most popular colours, then conducted another round of voting. The reward was a 79 percent majority in favour of petroleum blue (smart but good at disguising most workplace stains). Another irritation was safely out of the way. "Once again, it was a small but significant change. The best thing was that the employees decided. You could feel levels of trust and responsibility rise. People were happy."

Another hot topic was annual leave. Management used to arrange "bridge days"; if there was a public holiday on a Thursday, the company would give employees the Friday off as well, and then compensate for that with a working Saturday later on. This was unpopular. "*Deixa com nóis*" (Leave it with us), said the third Semco worker's commission to be created. The solution was a six-year plan for all holidays, bridge days, and compensation days. It may not have pleased everyone, but as soon as it was implemented, the complaining stopped.

Next in the firing line was the rule book. They began to eliminate set procedures, status symbols and privileges. This ensured that power was transferred to employees. It started with symbolic things like banning the time-clock and personal parking spaces. Each little adjustment seemed to help, and the feeling of trust increased. "Employees were surprised that Semco seemed to be listening so well. This was our chance to explain why we were transforming the business. We told workers that we wanted to make sure everyone enjoyed their work, we wanted to do better business, and we wanted to make more money. When the employees saw that we were sharing our vision, they brought us suggestions. It was time to take the big steps towards a truly humane workplace."

It became clear that the hierarchical paradigm was affecting motivation. Semler and Bojikian wanted inspiration from companies that had faced similar situations. They sent one of their employees, Joao Vendramin, in search of inspiring organisations. Off he went, with a Bucket List of his own. He visited Volvo in Sweden, WL Gore in America, and Toyota and Kyocera in Japan.

He concluded that the only solution was to dismantle the pyramid and create a network of teams. Employees should understand what was happening in their departments, and how they could contribute. Factories were split into independent units, small enough that employees were on first-name terms. Joao's plan was dubbed Amoeba, after the management model Kyocera pioneered. This calls for smaller parts, the "amoebas", in-line with the network-of-teams structure. Each amoeba had a maximum of 50 employees and operated independently. Some were obliged to relocate to other factories. These units still had managers but could be run according to team preferences. Head office should shrink by 75 percent, it was decided, and the corporate employees of the HR and finance departments provided support only when asked. Despite the costs, they went ahead. Their decision was not based on projections, but on intuition and faith.

The time was ripe for the next step: the dissemination of information. Weekly meetings were held where no subject was taboo. They talked about finance, new products and hiring and firing, all the while ensuring that employees became more and more involved in the business. "It was wonderful," says Bojikian. "Staff started to get involved with all sorts of matters. Their insights and their participation created a feeling of unity." Each day started with a brief meeting. Whiteboards displayed the financial and general situation of the units, and staff could judge their own performance. Ricardo Semler's reasoning was clear: "Nobody can expect anyone to be fully involved if they do not have access to all the information.

"And yes, I am familiar with the arguments against this. I was warned that during good times, our employees would use the numbers to ask for a pay rise – and fear for their jobs when things were tough. Maybe company secrets would be leaked to our competition. All of that was possible, but the benefits of an open, sincere and honest workforce outweighed the risks. We are convinced companies that do not share information lose solidarity."[37]

Keep people in the dark and they tend to assume the worst. Gossip becomes especially prevalent when it concerns financial matters. The truth is not always going to be pleasant, or easy to explain, but honesty and openness are vital. Every Semco employee received a monthly balance sheet, profit and loss account, and cashflow statement on their unit – once they had received rudimentary financial training to appreciate the information.

There was more to be done. "We decided to change the personnel review process, with employees reviewing managers instead of the other way around." Twice a year, employees had the chance to provide feedback via a comprehensive – and anonymous – questionnaire. Every leader received a score from 0 to 100, so they knew where they stood. The leaders who scored badly were not automatically fired, but there was pressure to adjust. "The most important finding was that visible improvement starts with a team conversation."

The next step was obvious. If employees could review their managers, why shouldn't they select them? And that's what happened. "Whenever we made progress, we would think of a new experiment. We wanted to search for more ways to keep our employees happy and strengthen the business."

Time for some more experimentation, then. Teams were given the freedom to decorate their workplaces, which resulted in colourful factories. And they set their own goals, which became more ambitious – yet more likely to be achieved – than those imposed by management. Flexible working hours become the norm. During our visit, Rafael, one of the factory workers at Itatiba, started late one day because he need to bring his child to school: "The best thing about Semco," he said, "is the freedom to do what you think is best. I did not feel guilty because I will catch up the time. I am not going to abandon my team."

Bojikian continues: "We also changed our hiring policy. HR no longer made these decisions – the teams were responsible. This not only ensured better selection, but also a greater effort to make new colleagues fit in. They could no longer point the finger at HR. But we wanted to go further and decided to make salaries known to all. A later step was that the employees could set their own."

KEEPING THE DREAM ALIVE

One vital question remained unanswered: what had become of the Semco dream? The changes had been implemented during the 1980s and 1990s, and since then, academics, admirers, consultants and journalists have shared the story of this exotic workplace. But most based their reports on sources around the close of the century. When we started looking for more recent reports, we drew a blank. What had happened during the past two decades? Was there anything left of the legend? Did they still work in the same way? Or was it eerily quiet because there is nothing left?

We put this to Semler. "At our high point, we had 5,000 people working at Semco and our joint ventures. I had proven to the world that

Superficial
as table
bean bags,
and free food
guarantee
workplace.

fixes such
football,
a bar,
don't
a great

this democratic approach is fine, in fact better than fine. I thought it was time to go in a different direction. Could a similar way of operating work in a different environment?

"That is why I now have a consultancy, hotel, and school that were all set up on the same principles. We must modify the system from the roots up, changing the way we raise and educate our kids. If we start there, the impact can be incredible."

In the 21st century, Ricardo Semler slowly sold off his shares. But, mainly for sentimental reasons, he kept the factory in Itatiba which we had visited, where it had all started for his father. That factory now had 50 employees; the other companies around 200 more. This does not detract from the inspiring story of Semco. Our long journey was more than worth it, just to be able to hear the stories of Clovis, Ricardo, and the employees and to visit the factory that serves as a tribute to the ground-breaking work.

After Semco, we drive to the coast and take a boat to Ilhabela (which in Portuguese means "beautiful island"). We enjoy the sun, the strong caipirinhas, and the nights filled with bossa nova. We stay for a few days, blogging about our experiences. We consider an important question: How do you avoid chaos in such an uncontrolled environment? Many people hear stories of progressive workplaces and assume it is a one-way ticket to mayhem, disorder and uproar. True, some companies adopt progressive workplace practices but fail to engender engagement. Often, that is because they overlook the crucial aspects.

Secrecy can be the enemy. Employees are clueless about how things function, and what strategy they are meant to follow. The only real communication from leaders amounts to corporate propaganda. All this results in information asymmetry. This imbalance creates all sorts of negative effects.

The dividends of secrecy are distrust, ignorance, gossip, and poor performance. How can we be involved when we don't know the result of our efforts? How can you have faith in leaders who limit access to the truth? What decisions can you take when essential information is not shared? In these situations, there isn't much opportunity to make reasonable decisions; think back to the iceberg of ignorance.

Radical transparency is vital. We have seen at Semco, and elsewhere, that as trust increases, involvement rises, people take better decisions. All key information should be made public. We enjoy the last rays of Brazilian sun and look forward to our next trip. Our target company is different to Semco in many ways. It is not about reinvention or getting rid of an archaic, dusty way of working, but we're quietly confident there will be some parallels and similarities.
It's time to return to London.

A SAFE BET

We walk through the city on an unusually sunny English day and reach St Katharine Docks, close to Tower Bridge. It's a joyful sight: sailing dinghies and small yachts are bobbing in the sun-dappled water. The former dockyard is now a collection of luxury apartments and offices – including the head office of betting exchange company Smarkets. Our expectations are high: Smarkets is one of the few places where self-managing teams, radical transparency and self-set salaries are the norm. We can't wait to find out more.

Smarkets was founded in 2008 by Jason Trost. It has offices in the UK, America, and Malta. Most of the 120 employees are based in London. The company doesn't offer casino games, poker, or bingo. Smarkets is all about event betting via a peer-to-peer exchange, where people can wager on outcomes. In 2017, Smarkets came second in *The Sunday Times* Tech Track 100, a list of Britain's fastest-growing technology companies.

We are welcomed by Celine Crawford, chief communications officer. We receive the grand tour of the modern office, spot a game room, and walk through the area where free lunches are served. We have seen so many progressive companies that we are no longer charmed by the stereotypical start-up culture. Superficial fixes such as table football, bean bags, a bar, and free food don't guarantee a great workplace. Pseudo-progressives can implement these things but fail to address any of the real issues, such as leadership, hierarchy, and the lack of freedom and trust. We came to London in search of the real deal, and we're curious to see if we'd find it. We meet a diverse group of employees: software engineers, the chef, communication staff – and CEO Jason Trost. We ask Trost about his inspiration.

"I wanted to challenge the status quo — not only in our industry, but also in the way businesses are run," he says. "I became heavily motivated by pioneers such as Valve and Zappos, and enjoyed *Reinventing Organisations* by Frederic Laloux. Based on such alternative workplace views, we started to experiment." Using the same continuous experiment-and-adapt method as at Semco, Smarkets has developed into a workplace that boasts many of the eight trends we value so highly. Its employees (65 percent of whom are engineers) work in self-managing teams. Each has its own functional focus: back-end development, finance and HR. Then there is a leadership group. The teams consist of five to eight people – small enough to move quickly, where everyone knows who is working on what. It is also big enough to provide diversity in skills and peer-to-peer learning. Free counselling is available for staff to share, and deal with, professional or personal issues. Peer-to-peer feedback is encouraged, and employees receive special training to improve their communication skills. Each team decides how it wants to work; there is a large degree of autonomy.

Some teams select their leader in a democratic way, some rotate the role, and others are leaderless. This is a common feature of true progressives. There is no set way of working, or a fixed list of mandated practices from support departments. It is constantly evolving. Unfortunately, autonomy is frequently overlooked. One of the pitfalls is that companies turn to fixed, off-the-shelf solutions such as Agile Scrum and Holacracy. Others copy-and-paste models from companies such as Spotify. They force their teams to work exactly as the new method dictates but forget the principles on which they are based. While the intentions may be good, the outcome is often top-down decision-making and reduced freedom. True progressives share authority. They create a workplace that is more than a façade of fancy ideals.

Talking to many of Smarket's employees, we learn about the weekly alignment meetings, where team delegates co-ordinate which team does what. A lot of people move from team to team. This creates transparency and prevents silo-forming. Internally, employees communicate transparently via a tool called Slack. All company financial information is available in real time.

Chef Alex Tsoflias explains the value of transparency: "Like everybody else at Smarkets, I have access to financials and the goals; and I can view all salary information." CEO Trost adds: "We hold regular town-hall meetings to discuss the most important developments. But maybe the greatest benefits come from the Q&A sessions.

"We allow people to pose their questions beforehand. They can do so anonymously. We would rather they didn't, but for some topics people prefer to." Just as at UKTV, people don't talk around difficult issues. The tricky questions are dealt with as well as routine ones. "It's important that people feel free to ask anything. Recent recruits don't do this right away, but they can see the process in action, how their colleagues ask these questions. That makes it easier for them to participate."

Celine discusses another aspect of openness. "Early in my career, we would waste time trying to guess what colleagues earn, and how big their bonuses were. Don't even get me started on all the gossiping. This is how we got the idea of making everyone's salary public. We talked to employees first, and, understandably, they were sceptical. We set up a committee to decide the best way forward. The meetings were rather intense, because nobody had ever gone through this before. We had a review before going ahead."

Many progressives have implemented this policy. For us, it is a powerful factor. The process forces one to consider fairness. If salaries are not perceived as fair, there will be problems when they are disclosed. Withholding this information could be a sign that something is amiss. When salaries and compensation packages were revealed on Smarket's internal wiki, some people felt uncomfortable. After a while, these feelings dissipated, and the new system became part of the culture. People don't even bother to look at their colleagues' salaries anymore. Initially they want to know how they compare to others, but when it becomes clear that the division is equitable, they don't waste the energy. This is a little different at Smarkets because it has taken the next step, where everyone determines their salary.

How does that even work? How do you let people choose their salaries, but not award themselves CEO-sized pay cheques? The answer, once again, is trust and transparency. At Smarkets, everyone can put in a business case for a salary increase. The data include a benchmark against performance, market rates, and peer response. A salary committee of peers views this and provides feedback. After that, it is up to the individual to decide and the proposed salary is made public. Anyone who has a problem with the suggestion can give feedback. If they can't resolve differences, they take up conflict resolution.

Many progressives use a process like this to resolve conflicts:

1 Talk to the person with whom you are in conflict.
2 Do things still not work out? Bring in a mediator
that you both trust.
3 Still nothing? Get yourselves a panel of mediators.
4 No joy? Then it will be up to an appointed arbitrator
(often the CEO) to force a solution. This is seldom needed.

So how does Smarkets avoid ridiculously high demands? That's easy, according to Celine. "First, we trust our colleagues. Second, we have a salary commission that advises you and can apply pressure. But if you were to ignore their advice, there is another mechanism: your new salary will be made public. That is enough: people no longer ask for absurd increases."

Self-determination is increasingly prevalent. Smarkets uses the business case method with a salary commission to provide advice, but there are other ways of doing it. Some organisations have a predetermined fund to be divided amongst team members. Again, it is a matter of deciding what works best.

During our final conversation with Jason Trost, we ask him to elaborate. "It is a never-ending challenge to be as open as you can," he says. "Not just for me as CEO, but for our employees. It is difficult for people to confront one another or have tricky conversations. We focus on providing training in the process of feedback. That can take a while.

"For us it is a voyage of discovery: What works now may not do so in the future." Quite so. It's always a challenge to deal with change and give employees the chance to help develop the business. But even more important is an aversion to dogma. The dislike of a fixed way of working that you can pick up from any management book. Trost articulates it well: "I want this to be a great company. I don't want to adhere to any orthodoxy. I want to do what is right at the time."

I want this to be a great company.
I don't want to adhere to any orthodoxy.
I want to do what is right at the time.

— Jason Trost

TRANSPARENCY AND JOY

Studies show that higher levels of motivation are a typical outcome of increased transparency[38]. Openness is also strongly linked to joy[39], with people working better when their performance outcomes, and those of others, are made clear[40].

Salary transparency – the scary one, for many people – is also proven to have a positive effect on gender equality. Research shows that the difference between the salaries of men and women is less when there is transparency[41]. If everyone can see that the system is unfair, someone will demand correction. But many still don't dare to take this step. A recent study that canvassed 70,000 employees found that 64 percent of respondents felt they were underpaid – even though they were all rewarded according to industry standards[42]. Some felt so strongly that they were planning to quit. Salaries that are kept secret can lead to feelings of injustice.

PIONEERING PRACTICES FROM AROUND THE GLOBE

Radical transparency is an important characteristic of progressives. People feel more involved, perform better, have more trust and faith in their leaders. Some balk at this, but it can be achieved in various ways:

LEVEL 1 OPEN COMMUNICATION

Everyone should be involved in the process. A popular way to ensure this is to hold brief daily meetings where team members share what they are working on and can indicate where they need help. Regular commitment meetings will allow teams to discuss the coming week.

Social media channels can provide a model. Some organisations employ ready-to-use software such as Slack, Facebook Workplace, Microsoft Teams, or Yammer.

Leaders should be communicators. Town hall meetings can benefit from a transparent Q&A session (such as UKTV's "Black Box").

LEVEL 2 OPENNESS AS THE DEFAULT

Some progressives make all information public unless there is a very good reason not to. This open-by-default policy ensures that as many people as possible have access to relevant information. It brings better decision-making and a higher level of involvement. Again, there are tech solutions, such as Google Drive and Microsoft Onedrive.

LEVEL 3 TRANSPARENT PERFORMANCE AND GOALS

Make sure that teams and individual members can compare their performance with that of others. An online comparison table can create a healthy sense of competition. At Buurtzorg, the healthcare people we discuss in the next chapter, teams use this to improve the way they deliver care. Don't let transparency be limited to financial goals and performance figures. Make sure that the information motivates people to achieve a higher purpose. Think back to Patagonia and Tony's Chocolonely, where progress towards their purpose was communicated transparently.

LEVEL 4 OPEN-BOOK MANAGEMENT

At Zingerman's, we encountered a powerful way of working: making financials transparent. At its Roadhouse we took part in one of the weekly open-book management sessions. Two hours before the restaurant opens, all 30 employees discuss the results of the previous week. Revenue, cost, and customer satisfaction are all touched upon. Everyone gives their undivided attention and expresses an opinion. The kitchen porter was in the chair. He assumed responsibility and shared his feelings later. "At other jobs I was mainly expected to carry out my regular duties," he said, "but here I can use parts of my brain that I never used before. We all run the company – and I can make a contribution." It is important to train people to understand the numbers. If you want enterprising employees, they must know how an enterprise works – including the financial side. Without proper knowledge acquisition, transparency doesn't mean much.

LEVEL 5 SALARY TRANSPARENCY

Many ascend to this level because they simply do not want to withhold anything. There is usually some excitement at first. People tend to look up each other's salaries out of curiosity. This persists for less time than you would expect. If the levels are fair, it's business-as-usual. Australian Bucket List pioneer Ken Everett experienced this at N2N. "Once the mystery is dispelled, so is the curiosity," he said.

What happens if salaries are made transparent and people feel they are unfair? Well, a great opportunity arises to fix a problem and nourish trust and commitment. Oh, and by the way, don't think there won't be feelings of unfairness when salaries are secret. If people don't know, they will guess. How do companies go about opening-up? Some are bold enough to publish all the information and see what happens. Others invite people to reveal their salaries. If you publish your own, you have the right to see others. It starts with a small group -- but the multitudes follow.

CHAPTER 8

FROM JOB DESCRIPTIONS TO TALENT & MASTERY

We've travelled the globe, visiting inspiring workplaces, chatting with defiant chief executives, employees, academics, and entrepreneurs who refuse to follow the herd, ticking off items on our Bucket List and having fun as we increase our understanding. However, we've noticed that some of the most progressive organisations lie close to home.

One company has, for years, been proving by example that a radically different way of working is not only feasible but leads to impressive results. We're talking about the Dutch home care organisation Buurtzorg. We've had the pleasure of meeting key Buurtzorg people from all levels, and regularly speak to those who were there from the start, founders Jos de Blok, Ard Leferink, and coach Gertje van Roessel. We have interviewed people on the front lines, too: the district nurses who are responsible for the daily implementation of the neighbourhood care model.

Buurtzorg has become one of the largest homecare companies in the Netherlands, with satisfied employees and customers. This is partly due to the goal of delivering "the best care at home". And all this has been achieved without the need for a management structure. Over the decades, Jos de Blok and Buurtzorg have conquered the world. These days, De Blok is often invited to share his vision, and his public appearances have earned him a variety of nicknames, from "the care prophet" and "the high priest of small-scale care" to "the king of simplicity". He has been described as "one of the most important thinkers of our time" who "should be running the Netherlands"[43]. De Blok appreciates the accolades but doesn't allow himself conceit, because for him it's all about simplicity, not genius. The words "keep it simple" and "just be normal" regularly come up in conversation with Jos, who should best be described as "a regular guy" rather than royalty or priest. Each time we meet him, we find the same modest individual, dressed in black. Apart from a touch of grey at the temples, the impression is black, black, black. No suit or tie, just comfortable black jeans, black shirt, black leather jacket. Even his wristwatch is black. With his soft voice and light Zeeland accent, he quickly puts everyone at ease.

His message is always the same, with oft-repeated phrases such as, "It's very easy to make things more complicated, but it's difficult to make things simpler", and "Why make it difficult when it can be easy?". Our personal favourites include "I'm allergic to management speak, protocols, and policy plans", and "Managing is nonsense".

"You have to let people do their work and allow them to apply their talents," he says. De Blok has been sharing his wisdom and catch-phrases with anyone who will listen. The message has found receptive ears. During many conversations, he gave us his version of the Buurtzorg story, which began in 2006. "I was a director of a large traditional healthcare institution. I started out as a district nurse, and eventually managed to climb to the top — but I never forgot what I learned on the front lines. As head of innovation, I had to implement many changes, but my initiatives to reduce the regulatory burden on managers, and to introduce self-managing teams, were shot down. I faced a wall of resistance. The other directors wanted nothing to do with me, and it drained my energy."

De Blok knew things could be simpler, and in frustration resigned. Together with Gonnie, his wife at the time, the development of Buurtzorg began. Indignation and frustration were inspiration to them. "We'd had enough of managers determining how people should do their work," he recalls. "I was convinced that true professionals know when and how to apply their competencies, without the need for managers." This conviction served as the rationale and basic philosophy behind Buurtzorg. With two other nurses, Jos and Gonnie formed the first team in Enschede. The concept soon became popular, with hordes of nurses applying. Almost all shared the same frustration with the impersonal and bureaucratic traditional health-care institutions.

Just 14 years after Buurtzorg was founded, it has a workforce of 15,000 nurses, spread throughout the Netherlands. It now consists of more than a thousand self-managing teams of up to 12 nurses, responsible for managing their own districts. The teams are autonomous; they plan their work and hire their own colleagues. Buurtzorg is defined by what it doesn't have: managers, unnecessary policies, an HR department, or marketing staff. It applies as few rules as possible, has no promotion policy, no complicated titles, and no lengthy job descriptions.

In traditional organisations, employees are expected to follow rules to the letter and adapt to any new policies. These companies think that careers are progressing as they did decades ago: in a predictable and linear manner. And, of course, always hierarchical; until employees eventually reach their level of incompetence. In order to make a real career, you were obliged to climb the ladder. Are you good at sales? Become a sales manager. Have excellent developmental skills? Go call the shots for a group of software developers. Skilled at nursing? Manage nurses. Even though it doesn't really make sense, it is the default path. Companies remove the individual from an environment in which they excel and give them a role that ignores their talents, skills, and passion. This hampers motivation and commitment. The employee and organisation are now victims of this absurd perspective.

One of the embarrassing symptoms is the proliferation of ridiculous job names. Take a quick look at your LinkedIn timeline. You'll see a wild collection. From overconfident Chief blablabla Officers to popular but meaningless titles including CEO for the only person in the business. During our travels, we've seen the world's progressives break with these ridiculous traditions. Buurtzorg is an excellent example. Instead of focusing on fixed job descriptions, they develop their employees' skills. They are aware that when talents are used to the full, everyone will benefit. We call this "Talent and Mastery."

Employees are encouraged to discover their own talents and use them. Mastery refers to their continuous development. It's not about hiding or improving weaknesses. It's about building on what comes naturally. Discover your strengths, then your preferred tasks – and make these your own. Of course, this may seem obvious, but there are few organisations that adhere to such a philosophy.

Many people never reach their full potential because of job descriptions, traditional hierarchies, and a "silo mentality". A large survey we conducted in the Netherlands with research agency Markteffect shows that only 33 percent of employees use their main talents in their day-to-day work[44]. Truly painful. But wait, it gets worse. Only 35 percent of employees perform tasks that match their interests[44]. As Dan Pink told us, using your strengths is a great driver of motivation. If we don't apply our talents, how can we reap the benefits? Many organisations aren't aware that they are wasting talent.

It shouldn't be surprising that progressive businesses are constantly looking for ways to take advantage of the wealth at their disposal. Studies show that employees are 15 percent less likely to quit if they can apply their strengths daily and are eight percent more productive when they do use their talents[45]. Accordingly, progressives leverage this. One of their methods is job crafting, turning your current role into one that gives you more satisfaction. Research shows that job crafting increases engagement and work satisfaction and reduces burnout[46]. Once again, it's clear why progressive companies put their talented employees at the centre.

Let's get back to Buurtzorg and see how they put this into practice. It's all about simplifying matters. The company has just one small office with 50 people. In addition, there are 20 coaches who support the teams. There is hardly any supervision, and the intention is to hold as few meetings as possible. Back to Jos de Blok, "Here at

I'm allergic
to management
speak,
protocols, and
policy plans.
Managing is
nonsense.

— Jos de Blok

Buurtzorg we have no artificial hierarchy; all decisions are made after consultation. If we cannot optimally use our people's talents, this is a significant waste. Our professionals come up with new ideas. They generate thousands of ideas every day. The sad thing is that, in traditional workplaces, they are rarely taken seriously. People don't listen. But at Buurtzorg we do." During our conversations with the nurses, the philosophy of simplification comes up time and again. The goal is to simplify procedures, rules, and communication to provide the best possible care. As little time and effort as possible is spent on tasks that are irrelevant. Moreover, the teams work independently. Of course, they can always contact the coaches and head office for help, but ultimately, they bear full responsibility.

Gertje van Roessel, Buurtzorg's first coach, explains the guiding vision. "All our activities are closely linked to providing high quality care. There is a clear delineation of tasks that are performed by the teams, and those to be undertaken by coaches and office staff. Most are carried out by the teams, which determine their own working methods. They start by deciding how best to provide quality care." That, and ensuring that everything runs smoothly, is down to the teams. "Think of HR activities such as hiring and firing, performance reviews, feedback interviews, and onboarding of staff," says Van Roessel. "Also, more general tasks, such as renting office space, performance checks, finances, schedule planning, and acquiring new clients." All of this is organised by team members.

In most traditional places, these tasks merit the attention of special-ised departments. At Buurtzorg, only certain administrative, legal and financial tasks are performed at head office. "If required, the burden of administrative work can easily be taken over," says Van Roessel. The IT system plays a crucial role. It provides real-time insights into results, sick days, client satisfaction, and specific care requirements, as well as an overview of workload and holidays. All this information is reviewed against company averages. Each team has access to all data. This isn't intended to create competition, but to allow teams to communicate and provide necessary support and insight. Communication within the team, as well as with other teams, is controlled locally — the sort of task that would traditionally be executed by managers.

Nursing teams decide what needs to happen and who is responsible. This is determined not by job description but by competence. "Each team member has a clear description of their roles, and each role includes multiple tasks," Van Roessel explains.

We visit Burgh-Haamstede, a small town in the Netherlands, to better understand these principles. What does it look like when job descriptions are discarded and the focus is exclusively on talent and ability? Nurses Nel and Patricia welcome us to their small office, where simplicity and functionality are the guiding principles. There is no luxury here, and the cramped office could not be described as inspiring; the nurses couldn't care less. They are motivated by more weighty matters, and as soon as they start explaining how they manage their neighbourhood clients, their passion and enthusiasm show. They tell how Buurtzorg has freed them from their bureau-cratic shackles. "We finally feel we're in complete control. We're able to apply our talents, training, and experience as optimally as possible. Instead of having to deal with a frustrating bureaucratic system, we can do what we believe in."

Nel and Patricia outline seven roles. These include:

1 nurse
2 caretaker
3 rapporteur
4 developer
5 planner
6 team player
7 mentor

The role of the nurse is self-explanatory. The caretaker is responsible for office matters, and the rapporteur monitors the team's productivity. The developer ensures knowledge-sharing and adequate communication. The role of the planner is scheduling. The team player ensures positive relationships and challenges the status quo. They may ask their colleagues: Why do we do things this way?, or What were the greatest challenges we faced today?'. Finally, the mentor is responsible for introducing new team members, onboarding, and coaching.

Each team member must fulfil the role of nurse. The other six roles are assigned according to interests and talent. There are no set requirements. The roles don't rotate too often. "Our usual advice is to change every six to nine months," says Gertje. "This allows team members experience of the various responsibilities and engenders respect for others." Nurses often find these diverse roles enrich their working lives. Buurtzorg lets employees develop their latent talents. The resulting diversity is much greater than with clearly defined job descriptions that do not adapt to the work reality and the interests of employees".

NEARSOFTIAN PRINCIPLES

In Mexico, there is another company that flouts traditional rules. Nearsoft gives its staff the freedom to deploy their talents. It was founded in 2007, and its 300 employees are software developers who provide remote support to American companies from bases in Hermosillo, Chihuahua, San Luis Potosí, Merida, and Mexico City. When we sit down with co-founder Matt Perez, he outlines his rationale.

"We wanted to create a company that works for everyone," he says. "Our intentions were good, but we had no idea if it would work. Fortunately, we found the perfect inspiration: Ricardo Semler and pirates." Pirates...? "Semler and pirates have a surprising number of similarities," Perez explains. "Not eye patches and parrots; I'm talking about their work philosophy. Did you know that every decision on a pirate ship was made democratically? The pirate code was drawn-up by all crew members."

There are other surprising similarities between progressives and pirate ships. Alex Clay and Kyra Maya Phillips wrote a book on the subject, entitled *The Misfit Economy*[47]. Pirates were often former merchant ship crew, where they had virtually no input, no vote, their ideas were barely heard, and they had no ownership. The captains, whose role was to look after the interests of the owners, would maintain discipline through violence. This caused great dissatisfaction and eventually pirates turned the system upside-down. Ships flying the Jolly Roger valued democracy, equality, and shared ownership.

Pirate captains and quartermasters were elected. All agreed on a constitution which determined how the ship would be run. Loot was shared fairly, if not equally. The captain and quartermaster would take a slightly larger share — one-and-a-half to twice as much as the others. Compared with CEOs of modern companies, who often earn

189

Buurtzorg is defined by what it doesn't have: managers, unnecessary policies, an HR department, or marketing staff.

hundreds of times more than the average employee, even this disparity has merit. Captains only held absolute decision-making powers during combat; in times of peace, everyone had a voice. Captains could be, and often were, replaced.

We were starting to understand Matt Perez' inspiration.

But how was this reflected at Nearsoft? We spoke to several employees and discovered the company's lack of hierarchy. There is not even a permanent management team. Every five years, long-term goals are defined by all Nearsoftians, as they call themselves. One of them, Kimberley Lantis, tells us that her "boss" is not a person but a shared goal. "Success is determined by the response to a unified vision," she says. "Every action must bring us closer to our vision." Nearsoftians also share values which serve as guidelines but remain subject to change. The manner of working is equally determined by all employees. This brings out the best in everyone.

Whether it's the quality of the coffee in the vending machine or a revised profit-sharing formula, anything can be brought up for discussion. Employees can make an open appeal. This means announcing the things they want to change and allowing others to contribute. The groups that are formed are described as leadership teams. They may seek external advice or rely on in-house expertise. The greater the impact and complexity of the issue, the more extensively it will be covered, and the more people will be consulted. The coffee choice will be a lot easier than devising a new profit-sharing formula. Or perhaps not... But the bottom line is that there are no rules or conventional wisdom other than common sense.

When a decision is made, it will be communicated and implemented. Does this guarantee happy employees? "Not necessarily," says Kimberley, "but that's not our goal. There will always be people who are unhappy, but they can make a change and be heard. They are free to make suggestions." By joining a leadership team with a specific focus, members can follow their interests. The on-boarding process? Then you can contribute. A new profit-sharing scheme? Start a group or join an existing one. Some employees will focus on similar topics and develop one expertise; others have wide interests and become generalists.

And Nearsoft has other possibilities for pursuing and developing talent. In-house, there are no job descriptions. Matt Perez, for instance, is only CEO on paper and to the outside world — but he doesn't have more individual power than others. His title of chief executive is used solely to communicate with more traditional companies. There is a six-week on-boarding programme, during which recruits learn about the corporate culture. Attention is paid to discovering talents, outlining the company's way of working, and providing feedback. Twice a year staff come together for Teambuilding Week. They share ideas, work together, and unwind. Everyone is free to determine their training budget and how it is spent — with the support of financial teams.

This approach has proven effective. Nearsoft has been recognised as one of the top companies in the Great Place To Work rankings, certified as a freedom-centred company by WorldBlu,[48] and named best workplace for programmers in Mexico[49].

PIONEERING PRACTICES FROM AROUND THE GLOBE

How can aspiring progressives build on all this? We've seen how Buurtzorg and Nearsoft are organised. We've witnessed the practical applications and results that come with a strong focus on talent and mastery in the workplace. Here are five best practices we picked up along the way. As you may expect, we'll start with the basics and gradually work up to the more rebellious options.

VEL 1 IDENTIFY TALENTS

Many use a simple survey to discover talents and share the results. Templates can be found online. Surveys can also identify a talent gap. This allows reflection and insight into the current distribution of tasks.

VEL 2 JOB CRAFTING BY COMBINING ROLES

If you don't like your current job, there are other possibilities. You can quit, find something new, or simply suck it up and continue suffering. Then, there's an alternative called job crafting. In the literature, it's defined as "self-initiated change behavior that employees engage in with the aim to align their jobs with their preferences, motives, and passions".

Job crafting is about turning your current job into one you enjoy more. And not just for the fun of it. Research shows it increases engagement and job satisfaction and decreases burnout.

Our goal is not to have happy employees. There will always be people who are unhappy, but they can make a change and be heard.

— Kimberley Lantis

Here are some tips on how best to approach this. The process builds on your team members' talents:

A Create an activities list

Create a list of all the tasks a team needs to carry out. Record everything on Post-it notes and display them around the office.

B Merge activities into roles

As a team, develop roles from activities that are similar or closely related. For example, creating social media posts, sending newsletters, and posting blogs might be combined into a marketing role. Another role may be financial, and include activities such as forecasting and invoicing.

C Choose your role

Now have team members select the roles that appeal to them. Forget job descriptions, and make sure managers do not force things. Base decisions on intrinsic motivation. A proper understanding of everyone's talent is vital.

D Don't forget unpopular roles

What do you do with the unappealing tasks? There's one solution we like: get rid of them! Simply stop assigning these roles. When doing so, the following may happen:

Scenario 1
Nothing bad happens. Team performance will remain the same or even improve. Your team will still perform. These tasks did not turn out to be so important after all.

Scenario 2
Problems arise. This is proof that the role is important. The solution? Start looking for alternatives. Create a priority for your next recruitment phase. Select someone who truly enjoys the role. Alternatively outsource it or find someone in a different team who enjoys doing this work. Be creative. There'll always be someone who's interested!

In Dubai we saw a good example of job crafting. The emirate's Knowledge and Human Development Authority has transformed several internal procedures and processes. Responsibilities for work and tasks are now assigned according to interests and talents. Fitness enthusiasts received training and now help their colleagues become healthier. This approach has been repeated for artists, photographers, filmmakers, poets, and writers.

LEVEL 3 UNLIMITED TRAINING

Let employees decide how to up-skill. They can be trusted to make the right decisions.

At the Spanish online marketing company Cyberclick, we learned that employees decide their training budgets themselves. They can choose snorkelling or surfing lessons. Cyberclick believes that any training benefits employees and the company. No monitoring is required.

Bear this in mind:

CFO: "What happens if we invest in developing our people and then they leave us?"
CEO: "What happens if we don't, and they stay?"

LEVEL 4 SELF-SELECTED MENTORS

Individuals develop better when surrounded by people they trust. At the Polish IT company u2i — where all internal titles have been removed — employees can offer themselves as mentors and choose their own.

Another IT company, Next Jump, based in New York, has a buddy system, Talking Partners (TP). It involves two employees regularly discussing their developing skills and talents (selected by themselves, of course). Talking Partners soon became known as TP. This was nicknamed Toilet Paper. Why? Because these people help you deal with your shit.

LEVEL 5 INTERNAL PROJECT MARKETPLACE

Some of the most progressive organisations have established an "internal marketplace". In Denmark we spoke with Lars Kolind, former CEO of hearing aids manufacturer Oticon. In the nineties, Lars eliminated all departments, management positions, and job titles. Projects were the driving force. Based on their interests, people took on as many as they wanted. Every task became a project.

Join
the
Revol

ution

SEEING IS BELIEVING

SEEING IS BELIEVING

In the course of our adventures, we've visited more than 100 progressives, from family businesses and non-profits to government departments, from private to listed companies, small and large. Some have been around for decades, others are relatively new. All pioneered one or more of the eight trends, but none pushed the boundaries on all. Each had to discover its own path, and there is no one-size-fits-all model. It's more of a one-size-fits-one-model situation.

Our journey to some of the world's most radical workplaces has shown how progressives differentiate themselves. Some have transformed and freed themselves from the shackles of command-and-control. Recall the rebelliousness of the Belgian Ministry of Social Security and the radical, bold moves of whitegoods manufacturer Haier. Even dull and old-fashioned workplaces can become inspiring. It's always possible to hit the reset button. It may not be a simple task, and transformations may be accompanied by unexpected twists and turns, but it's a fight worth fighting. There are traps for the unwary, such as basing change on preconceived notions or following a beginning-to-end plan. The process is not linear and predictable, but rather a continuous process of improvement and experimentation. These questions may still vex you: Is there nothing that can be done if you're not the CEO? Do you just sit and wait? Is quitting your job the only solution?

The answer to that last question, fortunately, is no. Progressive ways of working are always possible. Pioneers have pushed the boundaries way beyond what might have been expected, given their corporate circumstances. We came across teams in large companies that select their own leaders, while the rest of the organisation has top-down management. We met with department leaders who have eliminated management layers in their part of the organisation. In the end, it's about finding fellow rebels and pushing hard within your sphere of influence.

We learned how this works in practice during a visit to Harm Jans, one of the 1,700 employees of Dutch online retailer bol.com. Its way of working isn't as radical as some of the other pioneers, but the method of implementing change is. The move comes not from the apex, but the base. Jans tells us about this during a visit to the company's distribution centre in Waalwijk, the Netherlands – where the finishing touches are being put to a new warehouse. Since its found-

201

ing in 1999, bol.com has operated with a flat structure and high levels of autonomy. It has become one of the most popular online stores, offering around 22 million products. It was sold to Ahold Delhaize for €350m in 2012. But with expansion, things became more complicated. Many companies fall victim to their own success, no longer knowing how to operate on a larger scale. Growth can be a catalyst for decline. Jans came up with some interesting options, inspired by many of the organisations on our Bucket List. He wanted bol.com to become a pioneer too.

Jans soon ran into problems. He was the leader of a team of 30 logistics employees, but not senior enough to have much impact. Setting out to convince top management to radically change bol.com's way of working was tricky; he pitched his ideas to the chief executive. He found no support there. "People were afraid to go all-in," he lamented. In retrospect, that may have been a good thing. But this was not the only hurdle. "Bol.com was not used to all-in-one transformations, and certainly not if the decision comes from above. The company simply doesn't work that way." Jans was forced to look for alternatives. "The only chance I had to get something done was to encourage my teams to experiment."

And that's exactly what happened. The meeting structure was changed, roles were redistributed, as were accountabilities. The decision-making process was modified. During experiments, bol.com tracked levels of satisfaction. Regularly, they would ask the pioneers a simple question: On a scale of 0 to 10, how likely are you to recommend this new way of working? This helped them to see if they were on the right track. Based on consensus, they would adapt. The driving idea was that if people were excited with the new approach, they would become its active promoters.

Soon something extraordinary happened. Teams that had not been involved caught wind of the process, and asked Jans if they could take part. "Many new teams were willing to start at the beginning and so I knew something was going on". Jans and his fellows set out to coach other teams. They helped them adopt the new ways of working. "It gave us the opportunity to iterate and improve our methodology and the coaching approach. The second wave of teams was more satisfied than the first, the third even more so." He decided to go one step further. More communication was needed. The pioneers started producing videos, writing blog posts, and giving presentations. An internal group of part-time coaches received training. By the summer of 2017, over 400 employees and 50 teams had joined. A year later the figure had more than doubled and, by the end of 2019, this had increased to over 1,200 employees (70 percent of the total) with 140 teams. There is greater demand than can be satisfied.

Jans has undergone some personal change too. He was recently appointed Lead of People and Organisational Development. What started as a simple experiment had grown into something that far exceeded its intended scope. Small successes have led to major changes. Initially, only the meetings, decision-making, and division of roles were under the microscope; now, the focus is on entrepreneurship and ownership. The company's very structure is being addressed. "We didn't design this transformation up-front," says Harm, "and we sure as hell didn't make it obligatory."

This is a story of the inspiring power of rebellion. It proves that you don't have to be a CEO to change working methods. Nor do you need the approval of the HR department. It is about inspiring others with your vision, inviting them to be part of the process and then acting. Provided you apply these principles, you can create your own movement and contribute to a better and more inspiring workplace. Most progressives use a similar methodology. It may be different from the

This is a
inspiring power
You don't have
change working
Nor do you
approval of
department.

story of the
of rebellion.
to be a CEO to
methods.
need the
the HR

syllabus taught in business schools, and it may not be what the traditional consulting firms recommend. But it's what we've seen in practice, over and over again.

PRINCIPLE 1: DON'T FORCE CHANGE, INSPIRE IT

People often think that change can be enforced from the top, with directors deciding who should do what. Everyone is expected to obey. However, there are disadvantages: many CEOs do not dare take radical steps, giving rise to half-hearted projects. With coercion you can expect sabotage, opposition, and frustration. Instead, find the rebels, inspire them with your vision – and support them. In Bilbao, we visited consultancy firm K2K where there is a unique way of encouraging change.

The first two steps are telling:

> **Owners and CEO go all-in**
The K2K team first ensures that all owners will commit without hesitation. The next step is to involve the CEO, who must be aware that standing in the way could jeopardise their position. K2K makes them sign a document to that effect. If they don't sign, K2K won't support the transformation.

> **Employees vote**
The organisation is shut down for two days and workers are given the opportunity to visit companies that have been through the transformation process. This trip is made without the consultants, so employees can talk freely. Then it is time to show commitment. An anonymous vote is held. K2K will only start the transformation process if more than 80 percent of employees are in favour. This radical approach has proven its worth, improving the functioning of some 70 organisations.

PRINCIPLE 2: CONTINUOUS EXPERIMENTATION

People often think it's a good idea to design an extensive change programme in advance, inducing a sense of predictability and control. In practice, these bureaucratic exercises are often all talk and no action. If the plans are implemented, there will be no room for deviation. Not agile. Progressives have a different approach. They don't get stuck in endless analysis, reporting, and contemplation of models. They get down to business. Fancy plans and expensive reports make way for action. A clear vision is combined with a simple plan. Experimentation and reflection alternate. If the experiment succeeds, move on. If not, learn from the errors and adjust course.

PRINCIPLE 3: CREATE A MOVEMENT

Unleash a revolution, making sure that others become just as enthusiastic as the pioneers. What starts with one team or a department gains momentum. If there's one thing we've learned, it's that effective communication is essential. Make sure the movement is visible and follow the results. With success, or even setbacks, enthusiasm will spread. To make the movement grow, consider creating and distributing blogs, vlogs, presentations, meet-ups, pamphlets, and online platforms. Be creative and use every tool at your disposal.

REFLECTIONS

That day in the Barcelona beer garden now seems a long way back. For four years we've been travelling and researching the world's most progressive workplaces. We've seen at first-hand things that, back then, we knew only from books. The frustration of our corporate jobs has long since dissipated. We now get to research topics that impassion us. We meet pioneers around the globe who are as enthusiastic about these things as we are. We work with them and learn from their experiences. We share all this with fellow rebels through our blog, this book, talks and workshops, and online via the Corporate Rebels community.

As well as sharing what we learn, we get the chance to put theory into practice. With the team, we help organisations around the world to become more progressive workplaces. We also trial the latest and most rebellious ideas at Corporate Rebels HQ. We let our actions speak for themselves and continue to push the boundaries. Experiment, learn, adapt – it's true for us as well.

We donate 10 percent of our profits to charities, NGOs, and projects that share our purpose. To orchestrate that, we established The Corporate Rebels Foundation, a separate and transparent entity. Our business decisions are made through the advice process – even when it comes to salaries. We are carbon neutral as we compensate all our CO_2 emissions through carbon offsetting programs. We experiment with new ways of working, setting ourselves challenges for improvement. We self-set goals; each month looking back at our progress, and forward to the next challenge. We believe in radical transparency in everything. Obviously, we don't have budgets or childish rules. There's plenty of freedom; we don't track hours or vacation days, and everyone can work from wherever they please. To push freedom in the workplace even further, we recently bought a campervan and converted it into a mobile office, which makes it a hell of a lot easier to combine work with kitesurfing...

With every new phase we enter, our practices evolve. Nothing is fixed, everything can be altered. If it works, good. If it no longer works, we try something new. We are not alone. More companies are searching for new ways to break with the status quo. There are signs that the revolution is truly under way. Even large corporates are trying to break with tradition, considering four-day work weeks and, here and there, cutting back on management layers. It's not just behemoths that getting on board, small and medium sized companies are joining, as are passionate individuals from all around the world.

The best thing about it? These are not just management thinkers and scholars, but people from all walks of life. Leaders, frontline staff, entrepreneurs, journalists, policy-makers and academics are all joining force to fight for better workplaces. We're thrilled to find ourselves at the centre of the action. Our blog is read by hundreds of thousands in more than 100 countries. Our online forum is a meeting place for workplace rebels. We speak on a monthly basis at conferences and work with companies to help them break the bonds of drudgery, transform their lives and improve ways of working.

The time for a true workplace revolution has come. We need to push through and make good on our promise of impactful and long-lasting change – and to make work more fun. You can join the revolution, and here's how...

1 SIGN UP

The stories in this book are the tip of the iceberg. You'll find more inspiration at the Corporate Rebels blog. Subscribe to our newsletter and you'll receive a list of our must-read blog posts, newest content, and latest updates from the Corporate Rebels community. Subscribe at: www.corporate-rebels.com/join

2 SPREAD THE WORD

Contribute by increasing awareness. Consider what lessons you have learned and decide what changes you want. Make others aware of your revolutionary spirit. Use the hashtag #CorporateRebels and follow us on LinkedIn, Twitter, and Instagram

3 BECOME A MEMBER OF THE CORPORATE REBELS COMMUNITY

Create an account on Corporate-Rebels.com. Share your experiences, solutions and inspirations on the forum and get in touch with likeminded rebels.

Visit www.corporate-rebels.com to register.

4 VISIT A REBEL EVENT

We organise frequent gatherings. Attend one near you. Check out www.corporate-rebels.com/events for more information.

You will
never
influence
the world by
trying to
be like it.

Sorry

incon

— we're

to

the

for the

venience

trying

change

world.

ACKNOWLEDGEMENTS

Naivety is bliss. So is ignoring advice. Without a healthy combination of both we would never have embarked on this adventure. Starting up a company without a business model is one thing, writing a book while you're at it is another. It's been a long and bumpy ride. Deadlines have been missed and the publishing date has shifted from March 2018 to February 2020. But we made it!

Without the tremendous support of the people around us, this book would not have seen the light of day. Thanks to the first believers: our parents and families. Your trust that this idea would turn out fine was far from realistic but has been downright essential. Your support throughout life has made us who we are. Big thanks to Anne-Karlijn and Ananda, for your belief in us. It's the best feeling in the world to have you two by our side.

Thanks to the crazy one bold enough to be the first to join the adventure: Freek-Jan Ronner, and those who joined shortly after: Catelijne Bexkens-Koopen, Ken Everett, Ellen Dick, Florine van Wulfften Palthe, and Bram van der Lecq. You're all making the world of work a better place.

Thanks to editors John Mann and Hal Williams, this book's lifesavers. When we read our version of the "final" manuscript in the summer of 2019 we had a sinking feeling. We knew we had a powerful story but couldn't find the right words. You two have been able to turn that manuscript into something we enjoy and appreciate. And we guess, we won't be the only ones.

Another huge vote of thanks to all the people who have been willing to share their wisdom over the years: the pioneers on our Bucket List. We have taken a lot of your time to interview, research, and learn from you. We feel honoured. Some of you are not directly featured in this book, but rest assured your wisdom has heavily influenced our thinking. We are forever grateful to stand on the shoulders of giants.

Last, but definitely not least, our gratitude to all those who have joined the Rebel movement: those individuals and communities that have supported us through reading, connecting, sharing, and contributing. Without you, we would be just another voice in the wilderness.

1. FROM PROFIT

2. FROM HIERARCHICAL PYRAMIDS

3. FROM DIRECTIVE LEADERSHIP

4. FROM PREDICT & PLAN

5. FROM RULES & CONTROL

6. FROM CENTRALIZED AUTHORITY

The Corporate Rebels 8 Trends

7. FROM SECRECY

8. FROM JOB DESCRIPTIONS

→ TO PURPOSE
& VALUES

→ TO A NETWORK
OF TEAMS

→ TO SUPPORTIVE
LEADERSHIP

→ TO EXPERIMENT
& ADAPT

→ TO FREEDOM &
TRUST

→ TO DISTRIBUTED
AUTHORITY

→ TO RADICAL
TRANSPARENCY

→ TO TALENTS
& MASTERY

BIBLIOGRAPHY

1 M. Hayes, F. Chumney, C. Wright and M. Buckingham, "The Global Study of Engagement," ADPRI, 2018.

2 Gallup Inc., "State of the American Workplace," Gallup Inc., 2017.

3 M. Huang, P. Li, F. Meschke and J. P. Guthrie, "Family firms, employee satisfaction, and corporate performance," Journal of Corporate Finance, vol. 34, pp. 108-127, October 2015.

4 S. Melián-Gonzalez, J. Bulchand-Gidumal and B. González López-Valcárcel, "New evidence of the relationship between employee satisfaction and firm economic performance," Personnel Review, vol. 44, no. 6, pp. 906-929, 2015.

5 T. C. Green, R. Huang, Q. Wen and D. Zhou, "Crowdsourced Employer Reviews and Stock Returns," Journal of Financial Economics, Forthcoming; 8th Miami Behavioral Finance Conference 2017, July 2018.

6 A. Chamberlain, "Does Company Culture Pay Off?," Glassdoor, 2015.

7 R. Dur and M. van Lent, "Socially Useless Jobs," Tinbergen Institute Discussion Paper, vol. 034/VII, March 2018.

8 D. Graeber, Bullshit Jobs, Simon & Schuster, 2018. c

9 B. L. Parmar, A. Keevil and A. C. Wicks, "People and Profits: The Impact of Corporate Objectives on Employees' Need Satisfaction at Work," Journal of Business Ethics, vol. 154, no. 1, pp. 13-33, 2019.

10 Y. Chouinard, Let My People Go Surfing: The Education of a Reluctant Businessman, Penguin Books, 2005.

11 Patagonia Works, "Annual Benefit Corporation Report," Patagonia Inc., 2018.

12 R. Sisodia, D. Wolfe and S. Jagdish N., Firms of Endearment, FT Press, 2007.

13 Nielsen, "Doing Well by Doing Good," The Nielsen Company, 2014.

14 L. Goler, J. Gale, B. Harrington and A. Grant, "The 3 Things Employees Really Want: Career, Community, Cause," Harvard

Business Review, 2018.

15 Deloitte, "Global Human Capital Trends 2016," Deloitte University Press, 2016.

16 J. E. Mroz, J. A. Allen, D. C. Verhoeven and M. L. Shuffler, "Do We Really Need Another Meeting? The Science of Workplace Meetings," Current Directions in Psychological Science, vol. 27.

17 M. Marmer, B. L. Herrmann, E. Dogrultan and R. Berman, "Startup Genome Report Extra on Premature Scaling," Startup Genome, 2011.

18 J. Wallander, Decentralisation - why and how to make it work, SNS Förlag, 2003.

19 Svenska Handelsbanken AB, "Investor Presentation," Svenska Handelsbanken AB, 2018.

20 Svenska Handelsbanken AB, "Annual Report 2017," Svenska Handelsbanken AB, 2017.

21 J. Harter and A. Adkins, "Employees Want a Lot More From Their Managers," Gallup Inc., 2015.

22 B. Szatmari, "We are (all) the champions: The effect of status in the implementation of innovations," Erasmus University Rotterdam, 2016.

23 T. P. Principle, The Peter Principle: Why Things Always Go Wrong, William & Morrow, 1969.

24 A. Benson, D. Li and K. Shue, "Research: Do People Really Get Promoted to Their Level of Incompetence?," Harvard Business Review, 2018.

25 F. Gino, Rebel Talent, Macmillan, 2018.

26 Y. Morieux and P. Tollman, Six Simple Rules: How to Manage Complexity without Getting Complicated, Harvard Business Review Press, 2014.

27 J. Hope and R. Fraser, Beyond Budgeting: How Managers Can

Break Free from the Annual Performance Trap, Harvard
Business Review Press, 2003.

28 H. Kroft and P. Venema, "Arbobalans 2018," TNO, Leiden, 2019.

29 F. v. Massenhove and T. Auwers, De collegas werken thuis,
Lannoo Campus, 2012.

30 A. A. Roy, "Work less, get more: New Zealand firm's four-day week
an 'unmitigated success'," The Guardian, 2018.

31 L. D. Marquet, Turn the Ship Around!, Portfolio, 2013.

32 E. Winquist, "How Companies Can Learn to Make Faster
Decisions," Harvard Business Review, 2014.

33 A. De Smet, G. Lackey and L. M. Weiss, "Untangling your
organization's decision making," McKinsey & Company, 2017.

34 F. Galton, "Vox Populi," Nature, vol. 75, pp. 450-451, 1949.

35 J. Giles, "Internet encyclopaedias go head to head," Nature,
vol. 438, pp. 900-901, 2005.

36 Corporate Rebels, "How Real Leaders Melt The Iceberg of
Ignorance With Humility," Corporate Rebels, 2018.

37 Maverick: The Success Story Behind the World's Most Unusual
Workplace, Grand Central Publishing, 1995.

38 D. Burkus, "Why Do We Keep Salaries Secret?," Forbes, 2016.

39 TINYpulse, "7 Vital Trends Disrupting Today's Workplace,"
TINYpulse.com, 2013.

40 E. Huet-Vaughn, "Striving for Status: A Field Experiment on
Relative Earnings and Labor Supply," Working Paper, 2013.

41 A. Hegewisch, M. Phil., C. Williams and R. Drago, "Pay Secrecy and
Wage Discrimination," Institute for Women's Policy Research, 2011.

42 D. Smith, "Most People Have No Idea Whether They're Paid Fairly,"
Harvard Business Review, 2015.

43 R. Bregman, "Waarom de baas van Buurtzorg de baas van
Nederland zou moeten zijn," de Correspondent, 2016.

44 Corporate Rebels, "The Ugly Truth About The State Of The Workplace," Corporate Rebels, 2017.

45 P. Flade, J. Asplund and G. Elliot, "Employees Who Use Their Strengths Outperform Those Who Don't," Gallup Inc., 2015.

46 M. Tims, A. B. Bakker and D. Derks, "The Impact of Job Crafting on Job Demands, Job Resources, and Well-Being," Journal of occupational health psychology, vol. 18, no. 2, pp. 230-240, 2013.

47 A. Clay and K. M. Phillips, The Misfit Economy, Simon & Schuster, 2015.

48 WorldBlu, "https://www.worldblu.com/," WorldBlu LLC, 2019. [Online]. Available: https://www.worldblu.com/certified.

49 Software Guru Magazine, "Best Places to Code," Software Guru Magazine, 2017.

ABOUT THE AUTHORS

JOOST MINNAAR

Corporate Rebels co-founder Joost Minnaar left his corporate job in Barcelona, where he lived after completing his Master's in Nano-science and Nanotechnology at the University of Barcelona. He travels the world researching progressive organisations, blogs about the discoveries he makes and advises on workplace issues. Joost is a Doctoral Candidate at the Amsterdam Business Research Institute (VU University, Amsterdam).

PIM DE MORREE

Co-founder Pim de Morree also started Corporate Rebels after saying goodbye to a corporate job. That was just three years after finishing his studies in Industrial Engineering and Management Science and Innovation Management at the Eindhoven University of Technology. Besides travelling the world and researching, he writes for the Corporate Rebels blog, advises companies, and gives keynote presentations to inspire organisations to radically change the way they work. Together with the rest of the Corporate Rebels team, he supports the growth of a global movement to make work more fun.

Made in the USA
Coppell, TX
15 November 2020

41430965R00132